YOUR SPIRITUAL GARDEN

YOUR SPIRITUAL GARDEN
TENDING TO THE PRESENCE OF GOD

A Six-Week Daily Life Retreat

PEGGE BERNECKER

ST. ANTHONY MESSENGER PRESS
Cincinnati, Ohio

Book design by Mark Sullivan.
Cover design by Constance Wolfer.

Library of Congress Cataloging-in-Publication Data

Bernecker, Pegge.
Your spiritual garden : tending to the presence of God :
a six-week daily life retreat / Pegge Bernecker.
p. cm.
Includes bibliographical references (p.   ).
ISBN 0-86716-716-5 (pbk. : alk. paper) 1. Spiritual retreats—Catholic Church. 2.
Gardener—Prayer-books and devotions—English. I. Title.

BX2376.5.B47 2006
269'.6—dc22

2005029281

ISBN-13 978-0-86716-716-0
ISBN-10 0-86716-716-5

Published by St. Anthony Messenger Press
28 W. Liberty St.
Cincinnati, OH 45202
www.AmericanCatholic.org

Printed in the United States of America.

Printed on acid-free paper.

06 07 08 09 10 5 4 3 2 1

To Jim, Justin and the holy gardener of my soul, God

O you who dwell in the gardens,
      my companions are listening for your voice;
      let me hear it.

                                        —Song of Solomon 8:13

CONTENTS

ACKNOWLEDGMENTS

To Lisa Biedenbach and the editorial team at St. Anthony Messenger Press, I am so grateful you believed in the possibility of this project. Thank you.

Rev. Bob Amundsen and the pastoral staff at Blessed John XXIII Catholic University Center in 2002 helped create the initial ideas for this retreat. To those amazing soul companions, and the retreatants who gathered that Lent, we shared grace together.

To my mother, who planted vital spiritual seeds in my heart, and my dad, who allowed me to follow him in the garden to plant seeds and tramp over neatly planted vegetable rows, your patience and encouragement have made all the difference.

To the mentors and companions I have been privileged to walk with who have guided and inspired me, with special acknowledgment to Donna Couch, Vie Thorgren, Aimee Farrell, the monks at the Spiritual Life Institute, Dave Denny and Ron Rolheiser.

To the many friendly readers, former students and soul friends supported me in this endeavor. You know who you are.

To the earth, green things, critters, gardeners and gardens I know and find irresistible, you have taught me the wisdom of listening and participating in mystery.

I could not have birthed this retreat without the generous love and inspiration from my husband and son.

And to the Holy One that continues to astonish me, may you blow where you will, and may I tag along.

INTRODUCTION

Enter into a retreat in order to respond to longings and questions you experience in your mind, heart and body. Cultivate stillness and presence in everyday life! Retreat to discover more intently who you are as God's beloved daughter, son, sister, brother, friend and lover.

Retreats call us out of the ordinary *chronos* (chronological) time of everyday into the experience of *kairos* (divine) time. On a retreat we may encounter our own curiosity, creativity, community, courage, convictions, grief, solace and inspiration. We enter into deeper communion with God, the communities we engage and inhabit, as well as ourselves. When we return home from a retreat, we discover more about who we are called to be in relationship with spouses, children, friends, family, coworkers and strangers.

Making and taking time for a retreat is a luxury. We may have the freedom to go away for a day, weekend, week or longer. But often, time is a luxury we just don't have. And yet, we still yearn for it.

But surprise! You really do not have to go away. With a little effort and planning, you can treat yourself to a retreat during everyday life. This particular six-week retreat is specifically designed to take place in the midst of daily life. It can occur individually, with a small group, or in a community setting. Whether you are a student, single, married or elderly person, you can fit a retreat into your daily life—even if you are already busy with work, school, social and family commitments.

The theme for this retreat is spiritual gardening. So much life happens in a garden! In the Old and New Testaments we learn that a garden is present at creation, during Jesus' passion, at the Resurrection, in Revelation and many places in between. Jesus often uses garden imagery to teach his disciples. Think of mustard seeds, rich and rocky soils, vineyards, fig trees, lilies of the field and buried talents and treasure. Many Jewish feasts occurred during planting and harvest time and brought Jesus into the cities to be with his followers. Today we may visit or plant a garden to appreciate beauty; to harvest herbs, fruits or vegetables for a healthy meal or to simply connect with the deep part of ourselves that wants to be in harmony with the rhythms of the sun, moon, rain and seasons. The manual labor we do in the garden can be bone wearying, yet richly satisfying.

When we experience visible results from the earth, we find solace and peace in an otherwise fragmented world. Gardens teach us disappointment when bugs or four-legged critters destroy hard effort and beauty. Growing something, anything, is a lesson in patience and love. Gardens fill us with gratitude. This retreat, *Your Spiritual Garden: Tending to the Presence of God*, is designed to allow you to discover the life-giving work that can go into daily living for six months or even six years when you grow into a deeper relationship with the Master Gardener, God.

As you explore and discern whether this retreat is for you, think of the retreat as a package of seeds. Visualize the picture of a healthy and attractive plant on a seed packet (you), and imagine the potential of the seeds within (you on this retreat). Allow this book to be your seed packet. See what might come to live within the garden of your life.

In the beginning you will discover a number of practical suggestions designed to help you prepare for your retreat. These are essential for a fruitful retreat. Additionally, with the help of some guiding principles, you will create a personal promise or covenant to God to last the duration of the retreat.

On each of the forty-two days of the retreat, I will invite you to participate in daily reflections, meditations, prayers and practices, which will allow you to tend to God's presence in your life.

Together with the Holy Spirit you will become a spiritual gardener of your own "life garden" (your soul) as you begin to plant seeds, tend to daily details, appreciate growth, prune what is unnecessary, and gather and share the rich fruits of your labor. Most importantly, you will encounter God already waiting for you in all moments of your day.

Finally, at the end of the retreat you will make a second promise or covenant that calls you to interweave the insights you received during the retreat into your ongoing spiritual practice. With transformed power and insight, you will give God permission to delight in your life.

To embark on your retreat, you will need to choose a six-week time period. Anytime is a good time! Lent works well, but so does the New Year, beginning in January, or a new liturgical year, beginning in Advent (usually the first week of December). A birthday, anniversary or even a time of transition can be a good time to start too! Please don't limit yourself. The time can be now if you choose it to be. You do not need to worry if travel or any other major obligations will occur during the six weeks. In fact, these can be opportunities for greater growth and challenge. The financial cost is minimal: this book, a Bible, a few supplies and a possible donation to a spiritual director or companion. The retreat will be a time for you to pay attention to what is already happening in your life. You will spend time nurturing yourself, listening to the still, small voice within—or loud, demanding voice—discovering how God is speaking to you in present time, here and now. Only your personal engagement and time will reveal the gift you will receive from this retreat.

Are you ready to become a "spiritual gardener"? Are you ready to tend to the presence of God growing in your life? Do you desire to live more fully, with more vitality, awareness and clarity in your life? Then let's go gardening!

PREPARATIONS

These suggestions are designed to offer you some assistance so that you will be fully ready to enter into your retreat. You may want to spend the week prior to your retreat reflecting and taking time to do the groundwork. If you were planning to plant a garden, you would pay attention to the necessary essentials so the seeds and plants would flourish!

PERSONAL INSIGHT

Reflect upon and record in your journal the following two questions:

- What hopes do you have for this retreat?
- What is the greatest desire you have for your spiritual life in the present time?

Consider your answers to these questions. Take time to clarify your expectations for the retreat.

RESOURCES

Although you really do not need anything extra for this retreat, you may find it helpful to spend some time identifying and gathering other self-reflective resources (books, articles, music, audio- or videotapes, journaling material). The public library (or your own), local church or a friend may have something for you.

ENVIRONMENT

Identify a sacred place for the retreat. Create a special area in your home or some other place that you can use for quiet time, reading, reflection and prayer. Weather permitting, you may want to select an outdoor area—perhaps a garden—as a possible alternate quiet place for part of the retreat. Don't forget to consider a local park, church, arboretum, library or coffee shop.

DAILY ACTIVITIES

Review your normal schedule of activities and plan time in each day for your retreat. You will not want to disrupt your normal activities, since the purpose of the retreat is to discover Christ and the presence of God in the midst of everyday life. But at the same time you will want to make some changes in order to fully enter into your retreat. What will that be for you? Are there changes to your normal schedule and routine that would help make your retreat more focused and meaningful? Think about your family, work, school and social activities. Take into account the time you need every day for food selection, meal preparation, work, entertainment, sporting events, exercise, meetings and everything else you juggle. Plan ahead for the time of day that you will spend with the daily prayer reflection and meditation. You may want to wake a half hour earlier or stay up later in the evening. Ask yourself: How will this retreat affect my interactions with others? What do I want to fast from during this retreat time that will allow me to experience more fully a sense of being on retreat? It might be that you choose to add or drop some activities.

FAMILY AND FRIENDS

Ask yourself: Who are the significant people in my life, and what do I want and need from them to deepen my retreat? You may want to think about the type of support, understanding, consideration and assistance you will require during the retreat and pick someone to share with based on these needs. Whomever you do choose, you may want to explain to them why you will be cutting back on regular activities and will need help in meeting responsibilities.

SPIRITUAL DIRECTION

Spiritual companionship is an important foundation for a successful retreat. While spiritual direction or "soul-friending" is not necessary for a deeply fruitful retreat, you may find that time spent with a spiritual companion can be incredibly life-giving. You can find a trained spiritual director to meet with in your area,[1] or you can choose another option: writing to a spiritual director via mail (an ancient tradition) or E-mail (the more modern version of the tradition).[2] Now you may wonder what mentoring, spiritual companionship and soul-friending have to do with you? In essence, a spiritual companion is one who engages with you in holy listening and discernment of God's presence. I invite you to experience your spiritual companion as one who greets you on your own particular spiritual journey, walks with you, prays with and for you and, most importantly, helps you discern and listen to your own story of God and the sacred unfolding in your everyday life.

A spiritual companion is not intended to be a therapist or even a social friend. A spiritual companion does not use the time with you to catechize. Instead, the time you spend with a spiritual director is truly for holy listening—hearing God in your everyday life. Within Christianity this rich and often overlooked tradition of holy listening and spiritual companionship began in the early church with the desert *ammas* (mothers) and *abbas* (fathers). The hope is that your time with a spiritual companion will be fruitful, rich and deeply soul-nourishing for you. Generally, you will meet for forty-five minutes to an hour.

During this time you may choose to reflect on the following questions or any questions of your own choosing:

- What part of my spiritual story would I like to share?
- Which specific dimension of the retreat theme would I like to delve into more fully?
- What is my focus in my prayer and daily reflections?
- When have I noticed God's presence and God's perceived absence in my week?

- What area of my life and spirituality warrants further exploration?

We all need safe places and people with whom we share our sacred life story of hope, grief and dreams. Spiritual direction is a powerful way to understand our own spiritual autobiographies, which are a rich tapestry of experiences.

SUPPLIES

Prior to the opening ritual of the retreat, you will need to purchase or gather three items: a journal, a package of seeds and a hand-gardening tool. You will need a journal for your reflections. You may desire to use a textured or bound journal, but a simple spiral notebook or folder with loose-leaf paper will also work. Some of you may not enjoy journaling, and you might resist at first. If so, allow yourself to go against your initial impulse and give it a try. Still, if you find that writing in a journal does not work for you, try to draw or express yourself in another way. Just reflect in some way: It is vital to the retreat experience!

Visit a garden center or plant nursery. Go to the seed section and choose a package of seeds that appeals to you. You will not physically be planting the seeds (unless you decide to on your own)—so be adventurous and choose a packet that reminds you of yourself or intrigues you in some way.

Finally, you will need to purchase a hand-gardening tool. Please do not skip this step—it, too, is important. At the garden center, nursery or hardware store, look over all the gardening tools. Do not make your choice from a practical perspective. In other words, don't buy a tool simply because you already need it for your chores. Choose something that intrigues you without thinking too deeply about a reason why. It might be a small hand tool, or something larger. Throughout your retreat, your tool will be a symbolic reminder and teacher.

When you have gathered your three items and created your covenant, you will be ready to garden and begin your retreat.

1. Choose a location for your opening and ending retreat rituals. (Please note that on Day 31: Gathering Fruit of Delight, you will need to clear your calendar and arrange for a day of play. If you need to substitute the order of the days that week, please do. Plan this particular week to work with your life. But please plan ahead. Do not skip the day designed for you to play and gather delight in your spiritual garden.)

2. Every morning begin your day by slowly praying and savoring the words:

O you who dwell in the gardens,
> my companions are listening for your voice;
> let me hear it. (Song of Solomon 8:13)

3. Conclude each day with a short review of your day. Ask yourself:

- When or where did I experience delight and disappointment today?
- How am I aware of God's presence in my delight and disappointment?
- How can I offer praise to God for constant love and presence?

4. Finally, please remember this retreat is meant to be life-giving and transformative. Be willing to trust the Holy Spirit if things change. Adapt and flow with what your life wants and needs to be!

CREATING A COVENANT

*They entered into a covenant to seek the L*ORD*, the God of*
their ancestors, with all their heart and with all their soul.
—2 Chronicles 15:12

What is a covenant?

A distinctive part of this retreat is the making of a personal covenant. Your covenant will help you define some of the spiritual practices that will allow you to focus on and experience the theme of this retreat in your everyday life. The faith tradition of Catholicism is rich with points of connection to help you experience the sacred. For your purposes, a covenant is an unconditional agreement that you will design according to what will best guide you in this particular retreat. What you are committing yourself to is not intended to be a test or a set of hurdles to accomplish, but rather a well-thought-out guide to offer a supportive structure for you. It is not meant to be a burden. Your covenant is about placing your daily life, your work or studies, and your intentions in the presence of a God who loves you without limits.

As your retreat begins, take time to reflect on the things that you believe will assist you during the retreat and then write your unique covenant to shape your retreat experience. To aid in your process, some suggestions follow that you may choose to incorporate. Many of these elements are interwoven into daily reflections and meditations and offer you the opportunity to put your desires into practice. Please read through these elements, reflect upon what you would like to make of this retreat experience and create your personal covenant. It is now time to really get excited about your retreat and enter into the next six weeks with a vision, purpose and desire. The promise you make within yourself will assist you!

COVENANT ELEMENTS

DAILY PRAYER

Choose an amount of time to spend in God's presence each day that invites you to be mindful of each moment. Every day of the retreat includes a meditation, so you may choose to simply set aside time for the daily reflections provided.

SPIRITUAL COMPANIONSHIP

Decide if finding a spiritual companion is appropriate for you. If needed, locate a spiritual director or choose a trusted friend you will spend time with "soul-friending." Determine how many times you and your spiritual companion would like to meet throughout the retreat. Traditionally, spiritual direction occurs every four to six weeks. For your retreat purposes, you may choose to meet with someone more often, possibly at the beginning, middle and end of the retreat.

SABBATH ACTIVITY

On Sundays (or any convenient day) during the week choose something special, perhaps unusual for you, that will enliven your retreat mode, nourish your experience and open a deeper space for God. Maybe it will be a favorite hobby, a long quiet walk, a hot bath, an unexpected nap, playing a musical instrument, hiking, writing, cooking (or not!), a date with friends, a spontaneous trip for ice cream where you mindfully enjoy your treat or a visit to a park, garden or arboretum. Whatever you choose, make it meaningful to you and something that will allow you to be re-created in the Holy One.

EUCHARIST

Eucharist is the foundation of the Catholic faith tradition. Choose when you will participate in Mass beyond your usual Sunday attendance. This will renew and uphold your sense of the sacred and bring you into a deeper relationship with the community. If attendance at Mass is not part of your life right now, meet with close friends to break bread or share a meal.

PHYSICAL MOVEMENT

We live in our bodies. Too often we experience disconnection from this very gift that allows us to experience the world around us and express who we are. Decide what energizes you. Perhaps you desire a short simple walk or brief stretch each day. Maybe you prefer manual labor—like gardening—or dance and movement. Or do you have a favorite sport or activity that you want to participate in? Find something and get active!

FASTING

Fasting is the intentional refraining from something in order to open up space for God to transform us. Choose what you would like to fast from every day. Consider the patterns that keep you from deep relationship with God and those around you, and creatively choose your fast. It may be from a food, television, your hectic pace or perhaps harsh language and self-criticism. It may change from week to week!

RECONCILIATION

Agree to seek out reconciliation in a way that will open you up and help free you from anything that may be blocking your experience of discovering Christ within yourself or others. Plan to do this in a meaningful way. Confess to a priest or communicate with someone who has caused you harm (or whom you have harmed in some way), and in either instance seek reconciliation and forgiveness.

SERVICE

Serving others is a powerful gift to others and God. Think of a way you can serve others during this retreat. Perhaps it is undivided, deliberate attention to a spouse, child, sibling, friend, roommate or parent. Maybe you would like to volunteer at a local service agency, offer yourself to be in direct contact with a person or persons who are poor or marginalized or simply walk in nature while picking up refuse. How can you open yourself to serve another?

OTHER

Choose any tool or your own spiritual practice that you think would enrich your retreat experience. Be aware that you will personalize the elements of your retreat in your covenant. Be open to the inspiration of the Holy Spirit and be willing to change. Be flexible. The covenant is a support for you.

My Personal Covenant
Your Spiritual Garden: Tending to the Presence of God

They entered into a covenant to seek the LORD, the God of
their ancestors, with all their heart and with all their soul.
—2 Chronicles 15:12

I, _____, open my heart,
mind and soul to the movement of the Holy Spirit during the next
six weeks. I choose to give God permission to surprise me, challenge me and allow my heart and will to be moved to deep surrender, forgiveness and love.

After prayerful consideration I have chosen and commit to
the following acts that will help shape my retreat experience:

- Daily Prayer: _____

- Spiritual Companionship: _____

- Sabbath Activity: _____

- Eucharist: _____

- Physical Movement: _____

- Fasting: _____ _____

- Reconciliation: _____

- Service: _____

- Other: _____

_____

_____

I welcome what the Spirit brings into my awareness and life during these forty-two days.

_____

Signature and Date

OPENING RITUAL

*...we are not on earth as museum-keepers, but to cultivate a
flourishing garden of life.*[1]

—Pope John XXIII

Determine ahead of time a location to begin your retreat. You
will want to plan for a time period of approximately one hour.
Locate a place of beauty where you feel a sense of connection
with creation. You might choose your own garden, a park,
arboretum, botanical garden, porch or patio. Maybe you will
decide to float in a boat or canoe, sit on the shore of a river, lake
or ocean, lean against a favorite tree or park yourself on a blanket in a field. Try to choose a favorite place in nature. Ideally you
will be outdoors, but you may also choose a place within a
home, museum or other favorite indoor location. You determine
the time of day. Perhaps you will want to begin with the rising
sun or under a starlit sky. Choose the location for the opening
ritual well; it will set the tone for the next six weeks.

You will need the hand-gardening tool you selected (or that
seemed to select you), a package of seeds, a journal and pen,
and your completed retreat covenant.

Opening Prayer

*Spirit of the Living God, throughout these coming days I ask
you to open my heart to discover your presence. Plant seeds
of stillness and discernment within me. Help my vision and
awareness grow to discover how you are already present and
awaiting me in my daily life and dreams. Water me with gentleness and compassion. Prune away any unnecessary action
and hardness of my heart. Allow me to blossom with reverence for all of creation and allow me to mature in depth of
forgiveness, mercy and deeds for others. I trust you and bless*

you, granting you permission to transform me into your heart's desire.

Master Gardener, you created the world and desire that I love you with all my mind, heart and soul. Show me how.

Master Gardener, you are already present in every moment of my daily life. Teach me to discover and appreciate your presence in the people and places I encounter every day.

Master Gardener, you will come alive more fully in my life when I surrender to your loving will and design for my life that we create together. Allow me to give you permission to transform me into your ambassador on earth.

SCRIPTURE MEDITATION

Slowly read and meditate upon the following Scripture verses.

> They heard the sound of the LORD God walking in the garden at the time of the evening breeze, and the man and his wife hid themselves from the presence of the LORD God among the trees of the garden. But the LORD God called to the man, and said to him, "Where are you?" He said, "I heard the sound of you in the garden, and I was afraid, because I was naked; and I hid myself."(Genesis 3:8–10)

REFLECTION

God knows exactly where you are and invites you to come into full spiritual consciousness in everyday life. Where are you?

> Be still, and know that I am God! (Psalm 46:10a)

REFLECTION WITH A GARDENING TOOL

Pick up your gardening tool. Within your hands you hold an instrument designed to work and create. It will come to represent that and much more to you over the next forty-two days. Allow this instrument to become a tangible image of the desire you have for a deeper, richer life, assisting you with answers to questions you may not realize you have and taking you to places you have yet to discover.

Look closely at your gardening tool. Where was your chosen tool made? Whose mind designed it? Whose hands helped create it? How is the earth used and spent in its production? What about it attracts and intrigues you: shape, color, purpose, design? Ponder how this tool can represent a hope you have for your retreat. Can it describe your life to you? Are you willing to be surprised by what the gardening tool may come to represent and what it may reveal to you?

Spend some time writing in your journal about any ideas or insights that emerge from your reflection.

Next, speak aloud to your gardening implement, as if it has a life of its own and is a close personal friend. Talk about your hope for your retreat. Share aloud what you are most in need of and what you desire in your life. Then pray this Scripture:

> Then he took a seed from the land,
>   placed it in fertile soil;
> a plant by abundant waters,
>   he set it like a willow twig.
> It sprouted and became a vine
>   spreading out, but low;
> its branches turned toward him,
>   its roots remained where it stood.
> So it became a vine;
>   it brought forth branches,
>   put forth foliage. (Ezekiel 17:5–6)

REFLECTION WITH SEED PACKET

Hold your chosen seed packet in your hands. Closely look at the image of the matured seed on the front of the packet. Read the instructions and planting guidelines on the back of the packet. How do these images and instructions represent you and what you need to do to mature? Open the package and take a seed into your hand. Contemplate one seed. How can that one seed represent the hope God has for you throughout this retreat? Sit quietly for as long as you desire. Record any thoughts you have in your journal. Put the seed back in the package and recognize that you are planting a seed of desire through your commitment to this retreat.

In conversation, pray to God for your personal needs, your retreat intentions, the cares and concerns you have for the world and gratitude you have for your life. Trust that what you share will be fulfilled.

> "Teacher, which commandment in the law is the greatest?"
> He said to him,
> "'You shall love the Lord your God with all your heart, and with all your soul, and with all your mind.' This is the greatest and first commandment. And a second is like it: 'You shall love your neighbor as yourself.' On these two commandments hang all the law and the prophets."
> (Matthew 22:36–40)

During the days and nights of your retreat, you will be giving God permission to teach you to love more completely. Your reflections, meditations and actions will open you to experience the abundance of life.

COVENANT OFFERING

Slowly read your covenant as an offering to God and make a promise in your own words to fulfill your retreat intentions. Acknowledge that throughout the weeks of your retreat you may discover that some things may change and other things may be added. Determine a meaningful place in your home to keep your covenant, gardening tool and seed packet so that they may become important touchstones for your retreat.

Pray with the words of Blessed Pope John XXIII: "...we are not on earth as museum-keepers, but to cultivate a flourishing garden of life."[2] Sit in silence for three minutes looking around you. Use your senses. What do you see, hear, feel, touch and smell? Show up for your life. It is the only one you get to live. Write in your journal about any insights or questions you become aware of within yourself.

PRAYER

May I enter into the next forty-two days with an open spirit to delight in the Holy Other some call God and discover how my life is a rich spiritual garden giving witness to love in the world. Amen.

WEEK ONE: GROUND OF MY GARDEN

God is nearer to us than our own soul, for he is the ground
in which it stands, and he is the means by which substance
and sensuality are so held together they can never
separate.[1]

—Julian of Norwich

The LORD will guide you continually,
   and satisfy your needs in parched places,
   and make your bones strong;
and you shall be like a watered garden,
   like a spring of water,
   whose waters never fail. (Isaiah 58:11)

There are many types of gardens and equally as many individual spiritual paths. In nature we may encounter coastal or high alpine gardens and all the diversity in between. Some gardens might need to withstand severe winter freezing, and others require humid, tropical or temperate climates. Garden design ranges from formal to casual, haphazard and natural. Some gardens may be designed by specific color, flower, plant and crop types. A garden may contain flowers, herbs, fruits, vegetables, trees, shrubs and such natural elements as rocks, water and wildlife (and some tame creatures too!). A garden can be in full or partial shade or in the intense sun. Garden soil can be dry, moist, loamy, sandy, full of clay or even boggy. Wind and pollution add to the environment. Many gardens include decorative art, spaces to relax, supportive trellises and staking, or fences to keep critters in or out. No matter the variety or makeup, gardens are reflective of their environment, seeds, plantings, attention, light and water. So too are the daily lives we inhabit and live. And thus, so too is our spiritual life.

God created the universe and in chapter one of Genesis we learn, "it was good"! (v. 10). In the garden of creation are creatures of all shapes, sizes and colors, lands too multiple to ever fully comprehend, and an intelligence at the core that calls us to interior life and interdependence. Exploring the details of our life allows us to see more clearly and tend to the presence of God in our midst. Tending to God in our lives affords us knowledge about ourselves, while it sustains us and creates us anew. In a garden, tending to the soil and light ultimately provides the nourishment and ability for plants to take root. Like plants, we have places that we dig our life roots into deeply and that nourish us. At different times in our lives, we may take the opportunity to determine if we need additional nutrients, look more closely at the ground of what our life is "growing" in, and pay attention to light sources and the life-giving water available to us.

During the first week of this retreat, you will be noticing and naming your own specific life details. You have a unique life story with a divine thread weaving it together. The meditations for week one are designed to allow you to reflect on the specifics of the life you live and notice what is enriching and worth growing. If your life is a garden...in what type of earth does your garden grow?

PEONY

I have a particular fondness for Paeonia lactiflora, *the flower commonly known as a peony. For many years I desired to grow a peony in my garden but knew that the coastal climate in southern California would not support a plant needing a sustained period of cold in the winter. I rarely encountered peonies the first thirty years of my life living in California and only admired them through botanical prints, gardening books, photographs, paintings and a few childhood memories.*

After moving to Colorado, I was delighted to learn that I could grow a number of different flowers—including a peony! Right away I chose a garden location for the peony. But then I discovered hard, lumpy and dry ground. It was disheartening. I did some research and found out that a peony can live fifty years or more, and it was therefore necessary to take time to prepare the soil and location ahead of time. Paeonia lactiflora does not like to be transplanted. Not taking any chances, I watered, turned the earth, added compost and readied the ground for a warm fall day when I could finally plant my first peony. I chose a visible, sunny spot, so that everyone who passed it could enjoy the fleeting beauty of a peony in full bloom.

Day 1: Ground of My Being

For it was you who formed my inward parts;
   you knit me together in my mother's womb.
I praise you, for I am fearfully and wonderfully made.
   Wonderful are your works;
that I know very well.
   My frame was not hidden from you,
when I was being made in secret,
   intricately woven in the depths of the earth.
(Psalm 139:13–15)

The person you are today has been formed by many elements. Some you have chosen, others you have inherited and, for some, circumstances beyond your control have brought new elements into your life. From a catholic—universal—worldview, all of creation is imbued with the Spirit of God and holds potential and promise. It is from within this context that your retreat reflections begin. Openness to hope, faith and trust in the goodness and mercy of God brings fullness of life and unfolding of mystery. God invites us, through regular prayer and even the details of ordinary life, to enter into the process of our own conception.

You are unique, distinct and utterly irreplaceable. There is no other human person who has ever lived in the same way you have or who will live as you have in the future. The magnificence of God is alive within you and has been since the moment of your conception. A unique rhythm and identity that can be claimed only by you resides in your personhood. From the ground of your essence, you are known and embraced by the holy mystery we call God.

Although you may have had life experiences of loneliness, pain or even trauma, and God may have appeared at times to be absent, you have never been truly alone. Every human person is held in this inclusive and primary embrace of the Creator from conception. No one is excluded. Today offers you time to reflect upon the ground of your deepest identity, an identity conceived in God.

MEDITATION

Sit in stillness, noticing your breath and the unique rhythm of your heartbeat. Imagine yourself held in the embrace of your loving Creator. Enter into prayer with the *lectio divina* process (see guidelines below) using Psalm 139. Read the Scripture slowly, pausing in silence between each verse to ponder the questions and listen to your inner wisdom. Be gentle with yourself and allow any emotions and thoughts to simply rise within your awareness. Take as much time as you desire.

LECTIO (READING AND LISTENING)

Read the Scripture slowly. Rest in the words. What word, phrase or image captures your attention?

MEDITATIO (MEDITATION)

Read the Scripture once again. Sit silently. What meaning comes to you from the words you hear or the image you encounter?

ORATIO (PRAYER)

Again, read the Scripture. What rises within you that you want to speak to God about? Share your thoughts and feelings in a conversation with God, just as you would with any friend. Listen to any new awareness you may become conscious of.

CONTEMPLATIO (CONTEMPLATION)

Read the Scripture slowly. Rest silently in God's loving presence. Make journal entries about any insights or feelings that rise within you. Conclude by reading the Scripture one last time, pause, and then from your heart offer a spontaneous prayer to God for the time you have shared together.

Day 2: Ground of My Individuality

How beautiful you are, my love,
how very beautiful! (Song of Solomon 4:1a)

Each of us is born in a particular place, at an exact time in history. A part of our humanness is inherited genetically and other parts are shaped by environment and circumstance. Our personalities are formed from the moment we enter the light of the universe and are unique to each human person.

Some parts of identity cannot be changed. Race, ethnic origin and the time period into which we are born remain the same throughout a lifetime. Other elements may change. These include our physical ability, social and economic status, religious affiliation, likes, dislikes and even the ways we play, work and serve one another. We may be pleased or even frustrated with any one of the inner qualities and outer expressions of that identity. But, we discover our own identity as we learn to love one another and ourselves, and as we delight in the differences and commonalities of individual personalities.

Each person has a distinctive personality that brings a rich garden of diversity and experience into their families and communities. Belief systems, the culture one lives in and one's own unique life experiences shape and form the soul. All human persons have a beauty within that they express through actions and in relationship with others. God contemplates every person's inner beauty with reverence. God invites us to know each other and ourselves with the same sense of wonder and awe.

MEDITATION

To begin, sit quietly and simply feel your breath rise and fall in your belly for three minutes. Become attentive to any points of gentleness or tension you feel in your body.
Spend some time in reflection with these questions:

- I have personal characteristics that I inherited genetically. Are there five genetic characteristics that I like and five that I am not so happy about?
- I also have personal qualities that have developed over my lifetime. What are seven things I like about myself and seven pesky qualities that are like stubborn weeds in my life?
- How do I experience living inside of my own skin? Is my body a place of comfort, suffering, joy or ease? Has age, ability, disability or illness affected my life? Do I feel grounded in myself? How do I love to express who I am in my body—now and as a child?

To conclude, pause for one minute of gentle breathing and then, using your imagination, feel Jesus place his hand over your heart, look you in the eyes and say, "I love you."

Day 3: Ground of My Family Story

Like abundant leaves on a spreading tree
   that sheds some and puts forth others,
so are the generations of flesh and blood:
   one dies and another is born. (Sirach 14:18)

Within the human family every person is born into a family of origin and may one day create a family of his or her own. Throughout our lives we interact with other groups of people that are either related by birth or desire. Within the context of our family of origin or adoptive family, we experience a grounding of identity and a safe place to call home. Sadly, many people miss the opportunity of vital bonding at a young age. Others may spend much of their life in a family touched by tragedy, divorce or discord. Whatever our circumstances, we have a human family story that influences our identity.

A family story may include treasured memories and relatives. Cultural aspects of ethnicity and nationality may be strong touchstones. Our birth order and the places where we live and travel add dimensions to our story. Within each of us is a family dream and reality. Today will be spent recollecting the ground in which our life story began.

MEDITATION

For prayer today you will need your driver's license or photo identification card. You may also choose to gather any other important papers, such as a birth certificate, baptismal certificate, marriage license or passport.

Begin a time of silence for two or more minutes with this prayer:

Here I am. I come before you, O Holy God, to listen, to explore more fully the mystery of who I am, and the grounding of my life on earth.

Hold your driver's license or another important document that reveals on paper something of who you are. Gaze with new eyes at what you hold in your hands. Remember you are so much more than the words or images you see on paper.

Reflect upon the following questions and choose a few to write about in your journal:

- What is the full name recorded on my birth certificate? Is there a story to the name chosen for me? Do I have a nick-name?
- When was I born? Where? What are the names of my parents? If I am adopted, do I know the names of my birth parents? Who are my grandparents?
- What are three stories I remember from my early life? Do I have treasured stories from the life of my mother or father?
- Who are the other members of my family? Do I have brothers or sisters? Pets? Who are my aunts, uncles and cousins? What do I want to remember about them?
- Are there cultural aspects to my story that are important to me? Was a religious practice part of my heritage?
- What are happy and sad memories from my younger years? Where did I live in my childhood and teen years? Do I have a favorite memory from a home or outdoor garden I visited or played in?
- Have I helped to create a family at my present age? Who is included in my family? What struggles and joys are associated with my family of origin or family of choice?

Offer a simple thank-you to God for the life you have been given, for the things you have chosen for yourself, for the things others have chosen for you and for the circumstances that have occurred over which you had no control. God is with you, always.

Day 4: Ground of Permanent Commitments

But as for that [seed] in the good soil, these are the ones
who, when they hear the word, hold it fast in an honest
and good heart, and bear fruit with patient endurance.
(Luke 8:15)

Through personal choice or circumstances we have permanent
commitments in life that are made with visible or invisible vows.
A permanent commitment can be to a relationship with a
spouse, partner, child, particular vocation, organization or
social concern for the world. We can make an enduring choice
to live a life grounded in God's embrace. Our lasting commitments frame our future choices and freedom. We not only make
permanent commitments; the ideal model of permanent commitment makes visible God's action. God created a covenant
with us—a promise to be our God in spite of our sin and
betrayal. God's vow will last throughout all time, promising fullness of life, redemption and jubilation. Through God's covenant
with us, we are shown how to live in trust and permanence in
spite of hardship or suffering. We are blessed indeed.

Emotions and thoughts about our permanent commitments
can ebb and flow. Our permanency of heart is what matters in
the end. Permanent commitments can free us to love in ways we
have never imagined and can change through death, our own
difficult choices or the decisions of others. The effects can be
long lasting. The ending of a permanent commitment can be
devastating or liberating. How we choose to respond is what
makes the difference in our ability to either embrace life joyfully
or with resentment, bitterness and anger. In all of our permanent commitments, God invites us to generosity of heart and
single-minded love. Then the ground of permanency invades our
soul, softens our heart and allows us to love more deeply.

MEDITATION

Today spend time identifying and reflecting upon the permanent commitments in your life. You may consider gathering some favorite photographs of people you love and who bring energy and delight to your life. You might also gather any jewelry or other symbols that represent your permanent commitments. Light a candle, breathe quietly and just notice the symbols and how they speak to you today.

We all make visible and invisible vows to God, ourselves, others, places, things and organizations. In your journal record three or more of your permanent commitments.

For each commitment, ask yourself: Do I embrace this commitment with generosity, perseverance or resentment?

Choose three permanent commitments and write in your journal about how each is important to you and about the positive aspects you offer to these commitments.

PRAYER

Creator of the Universe, Giver of Life, in the beginning you created the world and it is good! Your commitment to humanity brought forth the birth of Jesus the Christ, who in turn sent the Holy Spirit, our Advocate, to be with us through the end of time.

Help me to perceive the life-giving dimensions of my permanent commitments and to prepare the ground of my heart and actions with a generous, persevering heart so that luscious fruits for the world may be brought to life through my visible and invisible vows and your promise of love.

Day 5: Ground of God in My Story

And when Jesus had been baptized, just as he came up from the water, suddenly the heavens were opened to him and he saw the Spirit of God descending like a dove and

alighting on him. And a voice from heaven said, "This is my
Son, the Beloved, with whom I am well pleased."
(Matthew 3:16–17)

Named or unnamed, God has been showing up in history since
the beginning of time and in your life story since your conception. Some of us begin to formally encounter religious institutions at an early age, even in infancy. Others make choices to
participate in religion at a later age, and still others experience
a deep spirituality separate from any faith community or religious organization. In your own life story you can recall times
when you connected with God and other times when the idea
may have seemed irrelevant. In all likelihood you would not be
holding this book and reading this reflection if you were not, in
some way, responding to a spiritual invitation or yearning for a
deeper spiritual connection.

Our spiritual journey has an energy that grows and matures
through our lifetime. In every world religion there are stages to
the spiritual journey that invite growth, personal responsibility
and commitment to a purpose beyond oneself. The nature of
God is to be generative and self-giving. From a Catholic perspective we are born into God's embrace and baptized into an
eternal embrace by a Trinitarian God mediated by Jesus Christ.
Many of us experience the sacrament of baptism at birth with a
decision an adult makes for us, but some of us experience it at
a later age through a personal decision.

Our God story is multidimensional and grounded in our own
experience. Formative people guide and inspire us. Paula D'Arcy,
a writer and retreat leader, recently said in a talk: "God comes
to you disguised as your life."[2] When we open our hearts and
minds to a personal experience of God amidst our everyday life,
astonishing things occur. We will gently discover that our God
story expands and influences our identity and ability to give
ourselves to the world with passion and purpose.

MEDITATION

Begin your reflection by offering this simple prayer:

O Holy God, you created me in a specific time, with your divine grace. Let me be aware of the ways you show up in my life and continually delight in me.

In your journal create a simple timeline of your life and make note of any of the following questions that appeal to you:

- Within the ground of my spiritual life, what are five or more key spiritual moments and people that have formed my spirituality and added to the richness of my life? Mark them on your timeline.
- When have you sensed or intuited a personal relationship with God as creator, mother, father in Jesus Christ or with the Holy Spirit?
- Reflect upon what was occurring in your life at the time. Were you in a place of consolation or desolation? How did the prayer encounter affect you?

When you are finished, sit in silence and focus upon the feel of breath in your body.

Offer a simple thank-you to God for your spiritual life, the people and situations that have opened your heart to God, and the many ways God comes to you disguised as your life.

Day 6: Ground of the Here and Now

There the angel of the LORD appeared to him in a flame of fire out of a bush; he looked, and the bush was blazing, yet it was not consumed. Then Moses said, "I must turn aside and look at this great sight, and see why the bush is not burned up." When the LORD saw that he had turned aside to see, God called to him out of the bush, "Moses, Moses!" And he said, "Here I am." Then he said, "Come no closer! Remove the sandals from your feet, for the place on which you are standing is holy ground." (Exodus 3:2–5)

Daily life is full of ordinary events and details from dawn into the deep of the night. We awake and move through our days with commitments, responsibility and delight. How we orient ourselves to the moments we live is crucial to our spiritual, mental, physical and emotional health. When we are able to engage in the daily business of living with an open, seeking heart we open ourselves to be available to mystery and the Divine, already present, waiting for us.

In the Scripture from Exodus, Moses was minding his own tasks when he observed something curious and stopped to observe more closely. His response to God calling him by name was to say, "Here I am." God also calls to us, inviting us to stop, listen and notice what is taking place. When we reflect upon the here and now of daily living, we will discern clues of precious holy ground in our own lives! An encounter with God in the present moment can occur and sometimes lead us on an unexpected adventure of grace. Identifying the ground of the here and now of our lives offers us the ability to show up for the hours we live with fullness of character, passion and intention, saying like Moses, "Here I am!"

MEDITATION

Take your shoes off and breathe gently for five minutes, paying attention to where your mind and heart wander. In stillness, use your mind to lead you on a prayerful walk through the hours and days of your life in the present time. Pay attention to where you spend a majority of your energy. Notice where you focus your attention. Ask yourself:

- What do I yearn for?
- Of what do I want to let go?

- Are there ways I feel oppressed or liberated?
- Does my life reflect the sacred dimensions of my personhood?
- Do I laugh and play often?
- How is the ground of my life precious and holy?

Record in your journal or express yourself in art or movement any insights that capture your heart.

Conclude by spending some time today playing in an unexpected way that brings delight to you. Offer thanksgiving to God for the gift of your life and all that it embodies, for you truly walk on precious, holy ground.

Day 7: Ground of My Garden
Place yourself deliberately in God's presence and breathe quietly, stilling your mind.

Take your gardening tool and seed packet and place them in your hands.

Slowly pray Isaiah 58:11, the Scripture that began your week of noticing the ground of your life.

Today you spend time reflecting upon your exploration into the garden of your life. Sit in silence for five minutes. Breathe quietly. Slowly review your week. Reflect upon your journal entries and daily questions of where you are experiencing delight and disappointment. Ask yourself the following questions, reflecting upon your life as it has been revealed to you this week:

- Where do I encounter God in my story? Am I surprised?
- What forms the ground of my spiritual life? Is the dirt rich, rocky, sandy, lumpy or impenetrable like clay?
- Has something worked well for me this week? What do I want more of?
- What type of garden does my life evoke in me? Describe it!

- Look closely at your gardening tool and seed packet. How do they reflect your retreat week and speak to your soul?

Record in your journal any insights, thoughts or feelings you experience.

PRAYER

O Holy God, Master Gardener,
you enliven and delight in me,
and I, with the multitude of
thoughts and emotions
that influence and guide my days,
take time now to see me
with your eyes of delight.
Can I trust your gaze
to hold only love for me?

Pause for a few minutes and rest in God's presence.

You, the Master Gardener,
are creating in me
a beautiful and life-giving soul.
Allow the ground of my life
to nurture well
the gifts you plant and dream in me.
Open the hardened rocky places within me
to be nourished by your penetrating
life-giving water.
Allow the clay that formed my inmost being
to be shaped by your loving desire.
And finally, dear Master Gardener,
may the naming and noticing
of my life details

bring greater glory and depth to you.
I offer this prayer to you with all that I am.
Amen.

WEEK TWO: PLANTING SEEDS

If we wish to reap it is necessary not so much to sow abun-
dantly as to spread the seed in fertile soil, and when this
seed becomes a plant, our chief anxiety should be to watch
that the weeds do not suffocate the tender plants.[1]

—Padre Pio

When a great crowd gathered and people from town after town came to him, he said in a parable: "A sower went out to sow his seed; and as he sowed, some fell on the path and was trampled on, and the birds of the air ate it up. Some fell on the rock; and as it grew up, it withered for lack of moisture. Some fell among thorns, and the thorns grew with it and choked it. Some fell into good soil, and when it grew, it produced a hundredfold." As he said this, he called out, "Let anyone with ears to hear listen!"...But as for that in the good soil, these are the ones who, when they hear the word, hold it fast in an honest and good heart, and bear fruit with patient endurance. (Luke 8:4–8, 15)

Countless seeds have already been planted in our lives! We become spiritual gardeners as soon as we begin to cultivate and appreciate the ways that our life can bear fruit and bring love into the world. Every single seed contains potential for development and growth, as do our life choices. In a visit to a garden shop or when leisurely reading through a seed catalog or favorite gardening book, we face a myriad of choices. Our interest in a seed is to develop the potential enclosed within its small interior.

Imagine you are planting a garden of your own. What questions would you ask yourself to determine what to plant? First, you would most likely determine the garden's purpose, which would influence your options. You might question: What type of garden do I desire? A perennial or flower-cutting garden? An herbal or vegetable garden? Maybe an orchard or berry patch? Will my garden be designed for my ongoing creativity and involvement or for simply a landscape? Perhaps you hope your garden will attract birds, butterflies or other wildlife. Once you establish your purpose, the ensuing choices become simpler. To decide about potential seeds and plants you would also consider: What are the light requirements? How much space do I have? Does the soil need amending? If fertilizer and amendments are needed, do I want an organic source? What about water requirements? Based upon all of these decisions, you would then choose seeds knowing the purpose or mission of the garden.

Each seed holds potential and promise; each seed is exciting! And just like each of us, a seed varies in size, shape and color. We place so much hope in a seed. Seed shapes appear round or pointed; bendable or hard; black, wheat-colored, brown, white or russet, to name a few. Some are so tiny it is recommended that sand be added to help with their distribution. Other seeds, such as sweet peas or morning glories, must be soaked overnight in warm water and even nicked with a sharp object to aid in germination potential.

We make a choice when deciding on the variety of seeds and starters to plant in a garden. Dependent upon the space and growing conditions, a decision is made for either a variety of plants or masses of the same plants. Our lives are like this too! At times we have large demands that take over everything. At other times there is room for more variety. In becoming a spiritual gardener we reflect upon the seeds we want to grow and what we value in everyday life. Seeds of life are our companions, commitments, obligations, prayers, play, the places we love, the unknown and the ways we give ourselves to others in work and through service.

With attention, all the seeds in our garden of life can flourish. When we don't thoughtfully consider and care for our seeds in our garden, the seeds will not grow.

Similarly, when you don't know the mission of your life, you tend to agree to too many things and then nothing grows well. You become frustrated, stressed and unintentional. Throughout this week of your retreat, you will spend time looking intentionally at the seeds of daily life—the things that already grow life within you and multiply on their own because of the energy and goodness that you generate. When you intentionally plant seeds in your spiritual garden, you want to pay attention to what you love, what you want more of, and what is most fruitful for your life and those around you. The seeds that land upon good, rich soil fertilized with prayer, perseverance and laughter grow strong and beautiful.

PEONY

A peony grows in my garden. Perhaps one grows in your garden too! I deliberately planted her from a tuber seven years ago in memory of my mother-in-law, who loved flowers, especially peonies. When Peony was placed in the ground, care was taken not to bury her too deeply. Peonies have what are referred to as eye nodules and a crown from which stems emerge in early spring. Even in very cold areas where the ground freezes, the gardener must be careful not to bury the eyes too deeply or the peony cannot flourish. We too are similar; if buried too deeply in life and demands, we lose our vision and ability to grow. This peony was most likely propagated by division from a parent plant, rather than from a seed, which could take from five to seven years for germination and flowering. I have planted Peony with care so that she may flourish for dozens of years to come. The waiting begins, with knowledge that she has life and blooms stored within, waiting for the appointed time to be made visible.

Day 8: Seeds of Life Companions

Faithful friends are a sturdy shelter:
  whoever finds one has found a treasure.
Faithful friends are beyond price;
  no amount can balance their worth.
Faithful friends are life-saving medicine;
  and those who fear the Lord will find them.
(Sirach 6:14–16)

A variety of relationships with people in our social lives, professional environments, families, faith communities, spiritual friendships and service commitments offer us an opportunity to feel interconnected with one another. The people we encounter every day and the new friendships we form interweave a beautiful tapestry. Yet in the multitude of relationships in which we participate, some matter more to us than others. Perhaps we are lucky enough to have a significant relationship with a person who lives nearby. Another relationship might have a physical distance or geographical boundary that limits face-to-face time together. Other relationships can be with people we no longer see or spend time with due to illness, death or other circumstances. We may have an important relationship with someone we don't know, but of whom we dream. We have a relationship with our own deepest soul identities and with God.

Each relationship begins with a seed of interest or desire. Then one makes the decision to continue developing the initial seeds of interest. Days, weeks and years may pass. Depth and comfort in the relationship grow. The seed of another's love nourishes, heals, challenges and supports beyond measure. Spending time with those who matter increases our commitment and trust. Eventually, we grow in our capacity to care and be a loving, supportive presence for others.

Today you will reflect upon the relationships that matter most to you and that have taken seed in your life.

MEDITATION

Center yourself in God's presence and become aware of your breathing.

Number from one to seven in your journal. After each number record the name of a person from an important relationship you value. Reflect about each name you write and ask yourself what you most appreciate about how the person has affected your life.

When you finish, picture each person in your mind's eye and offer the following prayer:

(Name of person), you bring goodness into my life.
I am grateful for you. Amen.

In the next twenty-four hours, if you come into contact with any of the people who entered into your reflection, tell them that you appreciate them and why. If you have time, write a card or call a person who holds a special place in your heart and life.

PRAYER

Dear God,
You have offered me the seed of many opportunities to be
in relationships with others. Open my heart and mind to the
grace and possibility within each person I meet.

Thank you for loving me through the hearts and actions
of others, and allowing me to love you when I love the other.

Day 9: Seeds of Play

I give you thanks, O LORD, with my whole heart;
  before the gods I sing your praise.... (Psalm 138:1)

One of the most valuable seeds of life is the seed of play! But it is also the most neglected. Play includes all the things that energize life. This is the seed of the senses. When we play we use our eyes to appreciate, admire, learn and delight. Our ears allow us to listen: to music, to wind, to rhythms and to voices of others. Our mouth offers us the taste of a mother's milk, a favorite food, a lover's kiss, the Eucharist. Scents evoke powerful memories, and our noses allow us to live in our body simply by inhaling air. In addition, through the nose we inhale the world around us, adding context to our experiences. Scents of fresh rain, newly turned earth, flowers, herbs, a favorite perfume or cologne, chocolate or crackling fire—all evoke seeds of memory. Our hands allow us to create, embrace and serve. Through our magnificent body we experience the world and things that delight us. We know God created the universe with pure brilliance! God breathed life into creatures, and the result is marvelous. How often do we spend time in pure delight with one another and creation, devoid of any agenda? Play is invigorating, affirming and results in a heart of thanksgiving and song.

MEDITATION
Begin by breathing slowly for two minutes.

Imagine you have a whole day to yourself without any obligations. Nothing is on your to-do list. For the next twenty-four hours, you can act however you dream and desire. No limitations exist. How would you spend your day?

Imagine yourself waking up. Where are you? Who is with you? How does your day begin? Moment by moment, allow your imagination to journey through the daylight into the evening.

Ponder: Who do you encounter? Where do you go? What time of year is it? What do you eat? How do you dress? With whom do you speak? How do you relax? Play? What do you long to do? For what are you most grateful?

In detail, describe your ideal day in your journal. Then respond to this question: What seeds of play and leisure nourish me?

End with a spontaneous prayer of gratitude to God for creating an amazing world that offers so many delights.

Day 10: Seeds of Landscapes and Places

Then God said, "Let the earth put forth vegetation: plants yielding seed, and fruit trees of every kind on earth that bear fruit with the seed in it." And it was so. The earth brought forth vegetation: plants yielding seed of every kind, and trees of every kind bearing fruit with the seed in it. And God saw that it was good. (Genesis 1:11-12)

We all have favorite places on earth. I have three at the top of my list. First is the beach in southern California where I lived for thirty years. Bliss for me is the textured feel of sand beneath my bare feet and the sun shining above while walking along the wave's edge and gazing toward the horizon. Second, our family cabin beneath a moonlit Colorado sky where the utter silence punctuated by owls hooting or the rumble of a passing train fills me with stillness. Finally, the Kenai Peninsula in Alaska has found a kindred spirit in the depths of my being as I encounter the vast, wild, untouched beauty and flowering fireweed. All of these places—and many others—evoke a sense of belonging and wonder, reveal clues about who I am in the world, and where my soul is nourished and revitalized.

You, too, have favorite places in the world that call to your soul. Maybe a favorite memory from childhood or the home of a favorite relative planted a seed in you at a tender age. Perhaps a favorite place is somewhere you visited during a service trip or on a vacation. Possibly it is somewhere you dream about visiting. Whatever the landscape, wherever the place, you possess the seeds of discovering the deepest part of you.

Taking time to ponder the landscapes and places that speak to you individually is not only interesting but valuable for your spiritual life—which is all of life. It is important to allow yourself to rest in places of renewal that evoke creativity and belonging and to invite others to join you there!

We often live in our deepest true self when we are in a landscape that we love and that may even rejoice in our presence. The world of quantum physics informs us that everything and everyone is in a relationship. Therefore, in a complex way, conceivably that we don't yet even comprehend, we are in profound relationship with the world we inhabit and the gardens we grow.

There are outer landscapes in which we all move and breathe and experience our being and inner landscapes to nurture and visit too! We pray in the inner landscape of our soul, but the outer world can bring us to prayer with utter gratitude, sorrow and thanksgiving. At times the world around us seems to rush in, and we are moved to prayer as effortless as breath. We are in communion with our inner and outer worlds. Focus becomes clear and the nonessentials of daily life fade away. We are awake in the present moment, more alive, more present than ever before.

What landscapes do you love? What landscapes do you think Jesus loved?

From Scripture and an understanding of the Middle East, Jesus most likely took delight in the desert sand and fields with horizons stretching into the distance. Seas, river shores and rocks seemed to have appealed to him. It was on a shore that he fed the multitudes, called his disciples, cooked a fish breakfast, and built the future church upon a rock named Peter. In desert landscapes Jesus challenged power, authority and temptation, discovering through prayer his own deepest truth. Landscapes bring us into harmony with ourselves and speak to us in powerful ways about what we love. Landscapes and places inform us about who we are, beckoning us to the unknown, the yet to be discovered.

MEDITATION

Take yourself on a fifteen-minute walk into the landscape where you currently reside. As you walk, notice the ground beneath your feet, what captures your vision at eye level and in the sky. Offer thanksgiving for the specific place you inhabit. If you are so inspired, find some unpaved earth, stop and feel the earth in your hands.

Think of who you are in this place. Is there anything that the landscape reveals to you about who you are now or dream to become? Is there another landscape calling to your heart and soul?

When you arrive home, in your own words, offer a prayer of gratitude for the earth and all it provides for you. Conclude by writing your own prayer of thanksgiving for the earth of landscapes, neighborhoods, earth, water, rock, stone, sun and moon. Slowly pray it.

Day 11: Seeds of Prayer

Then when you call upon me and come and pray to me, I will hear you. When you search for me, you will find me; if you seek me with all your heart, I will let you find me, says the LORD.... (Jeremiah 29:12–14a)

To pray is to desire God with all your mind, heart and soul. In prayer you become attentive to the Holy Spirit throughout the day and night, in ordinary everyday living. It is not as difficult as it may seem. Simply put, prayer is an ongoing conversation with a living, loving God. Prayer ebbs and flows, develops and grows throughout life. At times prayer can be a cry of the heart in anguish or ecstasy. At another time prayer can be a simple resting in the Real Presence. Throughout your life the ways you pray and relate to God will change. As a young child you were given seeds of words to pray with. As an adult you will move toward silent prayer, which will sustain you as you live your daily life. Wherever you are in your journey of prayer, the author of creation is always available, wooing you with divine presence.

People often say that they are too busy to pray or that prayer has lost the meaning and intensity it once held. I even hear the same lament in my own heart at times. This is not a bad thing! Prayer, just like any other relationship, changes, shifts, grows. What once was life-giving may become deadly. What once was unthinkable becomes pure gift. Desire for God is what matters.

Your prayer path will be like no one else's path. You are not the same as any other person. You are uniquely you and God knows this—you were created this way! Therefore, your prayer may appear different from the prayer of a partner or spouse, friend or sibling, monk or nun. Although there are expected, normal patterns and transitions in prayer, the practices that best nurture you will be determined by your personality and temperament, life experience, personal commitments and desire. Your intention and attentiveness is what enables you to pray without ceasing, in good times and bad.

MEDITATION

Take your journal and find a quiet place to be still. Breathe quietly for three minutes, allowing any thoughts to clear from your mind. Just be still in God's loving presence.

Reflect upon these questions:

- Who planted the early seeds of prayer within you?
- Where do you look for inspiration?
- Is there a special soul-friend who accompanies you through desert and darkness, desolation and consolation?
- Allow your heart to hear the desire of your current prayer life. How do you define prayer for yourself?
- Have you experimented with various prayer practices?
- Do you have experience praying in times of consolation, desolation or gratitude?
- How does your prayer life affect your daily life?
- What would feed you more deeply in your prayer life?
- Is there something more that you desire?

Conclude your time of prayer by entering into the remainder of the day breathing with the awareness of these words: *God is here.*

Day 12: Seeds of the Unknown

For nothing is hidden that will not be disclosed, nor is anything secret that will not become known and come to light. (Luke 8:17)

There is so much possibility in the universe. On conscious and unconscious levels we dream of what could be or might be for others, the world and ourselves. An ongoing conversation occurs with our future as part of our self forges ahead into unknown territory, becoming a beacon from beyond the here-and-now limits of time and space.

It is possible that the part of our self that pioneers into new territory is in intimate conversation and communion with God, desiring a not yet realized future. We receive inklings of the conversation through our dreams, hopes and desires. Seeds are planted within us, and if we are courageous and daring enough, surprising growth occurs. The requirements for growth are trusting life and realizing there is really no security other than love. So much possibility exists for each person, but possibility only happens in present time wedded with our willingness to engage in the world with wonder and reverence.

The seeds of the unknown are the most difficult to trust. Initially mysterious, we struggle against the unknown due to our strong human desire for certitude and security. If we are able to truly trust that God alone suffices, the journey of the unknown seed can be deep, exciting and real. We must trust, risk and go the distance. The deep true part of ourselves knows us better than we know ourselves. Dare we trust the possibility that it is in what we dream of for others and ourselves that we discover seeds of the unknown and God's dream in us attempting to be made visible?

MEDITATION

Find a peaceful location. Breathe deeply in the mystery of God and your own personhood.

If you put aside all of your commitments and the voices within saying, "should...but...dare not...cannot" for just a few minutes, what might you discover? Conceivably the spiritual seed of the unknown would be revealed in deep guidance leading you to richer, abundant life.

In your journal, number from one to ten. Then quickly respond to the following question, without editing your responses, with ten different possibilities:

If I could do anything without limitation, I would...

When you finish, read your responses prayerfully. Do you discover any similar or surprising themes? Choose one or two of your responses and reflect about how a part of your deepest being desires the truth that is revealed. What is it that you most wish God would reveal to you today?

In the next twenty-four hours, talk to someone who cares deeply about you and share the responses and thoughts that emerged in your reflection. Ask the person to pray for your continued courage to ask hard questions of yourself and seek answers.

PRAYER

> *O mysterious Holy One whom I bravely name God,*
> *teach me to trust the inklings and desires of my heart.*
> *Guide me to the questions, places and people*
> *that nourish your deepest truth within me.*
> *Allow my smallness to trust in your greatness.*
> *May I come to understand and love the generous dream*
> *you have for the one life I've been given to live—my own.*
> *May your grace and will be enough for me.*
> *Amen.*

Day 13: Seeds of Work and Service

For as the rain and the snow come down from heaven,
    and do not return there until they have watered the earth,
making it bring forth and sprout,
    giving seed to the sower and bread to the eater,
so shall my word be that goes out from my mouth;
        it shall not return to me empty,
but it shall accomplish that which I purpose,
    and succeed in the thing for which I sent it.

For you shall go out in joy,
   and be led back in peace;
the mountains and the hills before you
   shall burst into song,
   and all the trees of the field shall clap their hands.

                  (Isaiah 55:10–12)

Through our work and service we give ourselves to the world. In an ideal life work is deeply meaningful, contributes to society and adds value through creativity, accomplishment and purpose. For many of us, a large portion of every day is spent in a place of work. It makes no difference if we are a CEO, salesperson, educator, factory worker, caretaker, social worker, artist, healer or engaged in some other occupation. We all have an innate desire for worthy work, and we all suffer to some degree when we don't find seeds of meaning in our workplace. When we were young children, we dreamed about our future and thought about what we wanted to be when we grew up. We may have discovered what we were "born" to do. Or we may be disappointed by what we have become. Either way, we do not have to work hard to figure out a master plan. We just need to keep showing up for our life, the only life God has given us. God will bring all of our experience and talents together in ways we have never expected. We must dream our dreams, take steps to put them into action, and then be surprised by where God takes us!

How long has it been since you've reflected upon the early dreams within yourself—before the world may have intruded to define what you could and couldn't do based upon the privilege of gender, ethnicity, education, physical and mental ability, age, economics and other life events? Are there seeds of longing in the way you want to express yourself in the world through work and service to others? Have you discovered your passion? Are you able to live it fully?

In my younger years I dreamed of being a mother, writer and clothing designer. As life would have it, I wasn't able to give birth to my own children, and after many years my husband and I became foster and then adoptive parents. We now have one wonderful son. I also dreamed of owning a specialty boutique with clothing and crafts from around the world expressing a diversity of cultures. For a few years working in the fashion industry, I helped dress people up "on the outside." Then to my surprise, as my spiritual journey expanded, the dream transformed, and I spent the next seventeen years dressing people up "on the inside" in parish church ministry. I laugh with joy at God's sense of humor. When I was a young adult in college, a writing professor harshly ridiculed my writing in front of my peers. That experience silenced my writing voice for nearly a decade, until I finally returned to my undergraduate studies in English. Now well over a decade beyond that, I am writing my second book! The seeds that were planted in me as a little girl are blossoming, better than the way I had originally imagined for myself.

When in a work setting or in service to others—particularly the materially poor and marginalized—the giver often receives far more than the recipient in spiritual, physical and emotional gifts. The most profound form of service to others is simply showing up and being present to another, face-to-face. In the garden of God's love, the seeds of worthy work and service are inventive and life-giving for others, as well as for ourselves.

MEDITATION

Enter into the stillness of your breath and mind.

Sit quietly using the *lectio divina* process (outlined on pages 26–27) with the Scripture of Isaiah 55:10–12. Read the passage slowly, pausing in silence between each sentence. Be gentle with yourself and allow any emotions and thoughts to simply rise within your awareness. Take as much time as you desire.

Day 14: Planting Seeds

Place yourself deliberately in God's presence and breathe quietly, stilling your mind.

Take your gardening tool and seed packet and place them in your hands.

Slowly pray Luke 8:4–8, 15, the Scripture that began your week of planting seeds.

Today you will spend time reflecting about your exploration into seeds of your life. Slowly review your week. Reflect upon your journal entries and daily reflections about where you experience delight and disappointment. Ask yourself the following questions reflecting upon your life as it has been revealed to you this week:

- Where am I encountering God in my daily life? Am I surprised?
- Which seeds in my life are planted in good soil, among thorns, on the rocks on the path? Are there seeds growing in my life that have become weeds?
- Do I desire more of a certain type of seed?
- Has something new been planted in me this week?
- What type of garden does my life evoke in me? Describe it!

Look closely at your gardening tool and seed packet. How do they speak to you symbolically about a week of planting seeds?

Record in your journal any insights, thoughts or feelings you experience.

Prepare a meal today that will nourish your body and soul. Consider inviting a friend to join you.

Conclude by whispering softly in prayer to God whatever your heart prompts you to share.

WEEK THREE: TENDING THE GARDEN

*It was a great delight for me to consider my soul as a gar-
den and reflect that the Lord was taking His walk in it.*[1]

—Teresa of Avila

Then he told this parable: "A man had a fig tree planted in
his vineyard; and he came looking for fruit on it and found
none. So he said to the gardener, 'See here! For three years
I have come looking for fruit on this fig tree, and still I find
none. Cut it down! Why should it be wasting the soil?' He
replied, 'Sir, let it alone for one more year, until I dig
around it and put manure on it. If it bears fruit next year,
well and good; but if not, you can cut it down.'"
(Luke 13:6–9)

Tending a garden requires tools, time and intention. In tending
the garden of our spiritual life—which includes our whole life
since nothing is left out from God's care and concern—we must
make time to notice everything that is *really* occurring in our
lives and determine where our energy is to be spent.

In tending a garden, similar to the example in Luke 13:8,
specific plants may need more attention, while others are content to be left alone. The gardener may need to water the soil if
rain has not provided necessary moisture. Other actions might
include fertilization with specific nutrients, plucking weeds, cultivating earth, transplanting, mulching and even spending deliberate time touching, talking to and appreciating plants and their
growth, encouraging some along. The same is true for our spiritual garden.

The ground of the spiritual life is the very life we have been
given to live in the here and now. We must therefore spend time
watering our life with prayer, appreciation and quality time in

solitude and with others. As spiritual gardeners we need the fertilizer of love, friendship and meaningful work. Courage is needed to pull weeds of sinful actions and time spent in nonessential endeavors. Cultivating the "best" things in life requires discernment and our "no" to many things, even good things. We really only have time for what is the best in the ways we engage our time and relationships. A juncture may come when we discover we no longer have space or energy in our daily life for something we have loved, and as a result we understand the need to transplant a person, hobby or concern to a different location or to the symbolic compost pile of our life. We must identify the parts of life that bleed our attention and presence away from a primary mission and calling, learning to set appropriate boundaries that allow spaciousness, freedom and presence to erupt in our deepest center. Our intention must be to know what the most important things are so they may be put first, and our time can be spent in a relationship with that which matters most. Tending the garden requires hard work, but the rewards are innumerable.

Tending my spiritual garden has been the most rewarding and difficult part of my life. When living in California, I did not notice the seasons or my inner longing for color and growth as keenly as living in a colder climate. In California everything grew, and the landscape rarely changed. Thought went into design, light requirements and placement of plants. A trust existed that life would immediately come forth from dirt. And it always did, almost immediately! In some ways, the growing taken for granted resembled living an unexamined life. The visible landscape of changing seasons teaches hope and offers a keen appreciation of the growing process.

Because I have lived in northern Colorado for twelve years, I have a longing to gaze upon the color green every January. The earth teaches patience when bulbs and flowers hide, leaves turn from pure gold to brown crunch, then mulch, and light intensifies the dead-grass landscape. On a cloudless day a blanket of snow brilliant in the noon sun or illuminated by a full moon is beauty unparalleled. The soul rejoices in springtime when earth and all her plants erupt with buds and blossom. Possibility and hope are realized once again! An inner rhythm trusts the necessity of growth, flowering, letting go and hibernation. Seasons and the time of tending a garden reveal a great deal about how to cultivate a rich inner prayer life, the foundation of any spiritual garden.

As we tend to our spiritual garden, we first show up fully awake, take notice of the choices we make and of how resources of time, energy and finances are expended. Tending the garden requires paying attention to a quality of prayer life, availability to family and friends, how our bodies move in the world and engagement with the personal conversation God holds with each person. In particular, tending to our spiritual garden requires asking the daily question: *What is it only I can do with the time and space of my distinct life?* And then doing it with gusto, presence and passion!

An example of tending the garden in my own life follows. I have a primary conversation with the world through the sacrament of marriage in a permanent commitment to be a wife and mother. In addition, my lifelong mission or calling is to articulate God's love into the world. Over a time period of a few years, I realized that I was spending an inordinate amount of nights and weekends working in church ministry, and I had very little leisure time. The weekend family time I did have was scarce, and I often spent it at our cabin and had no social time interaction in town. I gained twenty pounds and had daily headaches. One appointment or chore ran into the next without question. After work I was often too tired to cook and grumbled to myself through meal preparation. Dogs became nice pets instead of cherished companions. I neglected my garden and flowerbeds. Life had become overgrown, and I was no longer a good witness to those whom I ministered. Relating to the example in Luke 13, I was in desperate need of digging and a good dose of manure to fertilize my life choices.

Through praying, writing in my journal, conversing with my family, close friends and spiritual director, I realized that my own "yes" to too many great things had created the unhappy mess I was living. With discernment I realized that God was inviting different flowers to grow and challenging me to reshape my garden. Slowly I began to incorporate a walk or yoga into each day. By waking a half hour earlier, I had more time for writing in my journal and contemplative or centering prayer. I began to schedule my son's sport games into a planner. I purchased a cell phone, so I could catch up with friends and family members during the long drive home. Still, the garden of my life was overgrown and fertilized in the wrong places. The best parts of me were not available to the most important people in my life. Sure, my work life was flowering and fruitful, but my personal life and primary commitments were still suffering. Desperate pruning was in order. The life I had created was choking me. Soon I decided to resign from parish ministry. I had to reconcile that I had one life to live, and I alone had to tend it well.

This week of your retreat will reveal and focus on what is really happening in your life. You will tend to daily time, resources, your physical self, others in your life, burdens and demands and the still, small voice within you. As you listen to your life speak to you, you will discern what shifts you can and need to make to bring you to deeper wholeness and holiness.

To tend any garden is to become intimate with what is planted and to trust in the process of growth. The work you do may be strenuous and even painful. But every gardener knows the results are worth all the effort through the fragrance, taste, beauty and joy a garden delivers into the world.

❀ Peony

Just last week I cleared away fallen leaves from where a pink peony lives. Pencil-thin protrusions of burgundy stems were emerging from the soil. I pulled overgrown oregano, chopped a volunteer scrub oak attempting to grow and gently removed the remains of last year's growth. Within a week stems rose six inches, and a very early bud the size of a golf ball formed. Snow added needed moisture. I worry that Peony will bloom much too soon and freeze, but the process must be trusted. A slight bit of mulch is added to her base. Spring is coming!

Day 15: Tending Time

For everything there is a season, and a time for every matter under heaven:
  a time to be born, and a time to die;
  a time to plant, and a time to pluck up what is planted;
  a time to kill, and a time to heal;
  a time to break down, and a time to build up;
  a time to weep, and a time to laugh;
  a time to mourn, and a time to dance;
  a time to throw away stones, and a time to gather
    stones together;
  a time to embrace, and a time to refrain from
    embracing;
  a time to seek, and a time to lose;

a time to keep, and a time to throw away;

a time to tear, and a time to sew;

a time to keep silence, and a time to speak;

a time to love, and a time to hate;

a time for war, and a time for peace.

(Ecclesiastes 3:1–8)

We each have a preference for how we engage in the world. Some of us are extroverts and gain energy from others, talking through ideas aloud, bringing God vitally alive. The extroverts of the world are recharged by activity and being with close friends, in the company of others. Although every human person requires a daily dose of solitude with just God, extroverts also particularly enjoy communal prayer and play with others. Some of us are introverted, bringing a thoughtful stillness and depth to relationships. Introverts are energized in the inner garden and need time every day to be in solitude where a rich inner life is revitalized and watered. How our personality has been formed is important in understanding how we relate to time, people and even God.[2]

In our spiritual garden tending to time means to show up for our life, fully engaged. We prioritize within ourselves what our most important values are in order to make choices that reflect what matters most deeply to us. We all have experienced agreeing to something but later regretting our choice. Being deliberate ahead of time allows us freedom to know that we are watering the actual garden, not wasting water on sand and rock. In addition to showing up for our lives, we can learn to trust that God will provide us all the time we need for our choices that are inspired by grace. A tremendous spaciousness opens within us when we invite God to help us choose where our energy can be expended. Then we act and realize God's timing is impeccable.

MEDITATION

Your reflection today will center on your relationship with time. You will need either your calendar or planner with you. If you use an electronic organizing system, print nine months of appointments: the past six months and the upcoming three months. If you already have a hard copy, gather your calendar for the same time period.

Light a candle and place a clock nearby. Sit quietly with your planner or calendar on your lap.

Slowly read Ecclesiastes 3:1–8 aloud. Close your eyes. For three minutes focus on your breathing and the movement of breath in your body.

Gradually bring your attention to your calendar. Gently review the past six months and upcoming three months. Become aware of where your time is spent. Do not analyze or critique. Simply notice and pay attention as if you were exploring your life for the first time. When you feel ready, set your calendar aside and breathe silently for three minutes.

In your journal, respond to these questions:

- What emotions and thoughts do I experience while reviewing my calendar?
- Did my breath shift within my body? If so, how?
- What needs my attention in a new way?
- What seasons or times have I experienced?

Conclude by composing your personal "for everything there is a season, and a time for every matter under heaven" (Ecclesiastes 3:1). What time is it in your life?

Day 16: Tending Finances

For where your treasure is, there your heart will be also. (Matthew 6:21)

We have a powerful relationship with currency whether we realize it or not. Our powerful money story and use of finances is a wonderful mirror to reveal our core values and invisible assumptions. Money is a necessary and curious commodity. Every person has a money story and relationship with treasures of the heart and riches of the world. What does money represent to you? Perhaps the answer could be security, opportunity, choices, power, options, status, success, education, credibility or an ability to enable or help others. A form of energy that we exchange, money can disappoint, excite or do both. Providing access or limiting choices, currency creates a powerful dynamic in our lives that we must acknowledge.

From a young age we receive dominant messages about the purpose and usage of money. Whether or not we comprehend it, we inherit a money story from our family of origin. Our western culture provides powerful money messages. Churches, institutions and workplaces offer further positions. A financial adviser or stockbroker might even offer additional perspectives. From a spiritual point of view, it is significant to recognize that each individual assigns a value and purpose to money. Therefore, understanding our individual money story and the meaning we personally assign to treasures of any kind is a spiritual practice. Our relationship with money may arise from a very different perspective from that of a spouse, partner, parent, friend, organization or government. Thus, our interpersonal interactions can be filled with conflict, neutrality or harmony.[3]

Tending to the garden of finances can surprise and startle us! Without awareness and reflection, powerful myths around money will unconsciously motivate our decisions and influence our interior freedom. The first step is to become aware of the meaning we internalize, give and perpetuate concerning finances and treasures. Today is a small taste of your beginning to tend the financial story of your life.

MEDITATION

Your reflection today will begin to engage your relationship with money. You will need your wallet and three recent bank statements with you. If you utilize computer software, print a monthly summary of income and expenses for a three-month time period. If you have a budget, gather that too.

Light a candle, place the documents nearby and breathe silently resting in God's presence for two or more minutes.

Begin your reflection by recalling the first time you saved money for something. How did you earn or receive the money you saved? Do you remember a special childhood bank? What messages did you learn about money from the people close to you? Sit quietly while you tend to memories of parents, relatives and adults interacting with money. Was there always enough, not enough? Allow any insights to surface.

Write in your journal for a few minutes about your thoughts.

Moving forward to present time, closely review your income and expenses without judgment. Pay attention to the thoughts and emotions that arise in you. Ask yourself: Are you surprised? Dismayed? Encouraged? Where is an area of perceived lack or abundance?

Journal again about what you notice and feel. Allow any thoughts to surface in your writing. When you are finished, reread what you have written. Choose one thing you would like to explore further. Write it on a separate piece of paper in the form of a question or statement for deeper consideration.

Now sit quietly with your financial accounting or wallet in your hands. Enter into the *lectio divina* process (on pages 26–27) by means of the question or statement you would like to explore further, or anything else this reflection has evoked in you as your sacred text for reflection.

Conclude in your own words by offering a prayer of thanksgiving to God for treasures, resources and the time you have shared together.

Day 17: Tending to the Physical

Do you not know that you are God's temple and that God's Spirit dwells in you? (1 Corinthians 3:16)

Gardening is a physical act requiring stamina. Hunched over a row of seedlings, planting, pulling weeds, pruning, hoeing and mowing all ask for physical effort on the part of the gardener for healthy growth and fruition. If you garden or engage in any manual labor, you know the experience of aching muscles and the contented relief of hobbling to a waiting chair or step at the end of a day, senses awakened, the body absorbed with activity. Arranging cut flowers, preparing a meal from a garden's abundance, walking barefoot in dew-tipped grass or simply admiring the beauty of nature uplifts the body and senses. Our life details can initiate the same response. Sometimes we are overspent and at other times utterly entranced and delighted.

Our bodies are magnificent, mysterious containers that age and offer ability, emotion, pain and delight. The body allows an experience of pleasure or discomfort and can take us to places that we dream about. With the passing of time we mature and change. Physical ability can shift slowly or suddenly with an accident or illness. What was once easy becomes an act of effort. Lines on our skin reveal personality and temperament. Emotions and memory are held in our muscles at a cellular level. The connection with our body is complex and exciting.

The culture we inhabit offers external messages about how we should look, perform and dress. Too often falsehoods are internalized that become the measure of our worth. In essence, without care, we can abuse the beauty of our created body by not appreciating and tending to our visible incarnation.

Every day it is important to engage in some type of physical activity and be mindful of how we feed our physical self. Fresh organic produce from a local garden feeds cells and life force. Processed foods with hormones and chemicals merely starve our cells of potential. Our physical body is a gift that allows us to experience the world with all our senses and interact with one another sharing love, compassion and God.

MEDITATION

Today you will tend to your body as you engage in daily details of living.

Begin by gently stretching all of your muscles. You know your abilities, so choose what is appropriate for you. Pay attention to your shoulders, arms, neck, back, chest and legs. Make sure to wiggle your toes and fingers. Notice any areas of tension or stiffness. Breathe into troubled spots to gently let go of any places holding tightness or strain. Allow your conscious breath to heal your tension. See if you can feel or observe the energy flow within your body. Offer thanksgiving for your magnificent body that allows you to take pleasure in the world, regardless of any current pain or illness. God is present in all your experience.

Choose from any of the following options or create your own for today's spiritual practice:

- Mindfully enjoy a meal. Offer a blessing for the earth and creatures that provided for it.
- Take a long, luxurious bath or shower and gently massage your skin and muscles with renewed wonder.
- Walk barefoot outdoors or play in nature in an unexpected way.
- Dress in clothing that allows you to feel alive and spectacularly yourself.

- Engage in a favorite sport or exercise.
- Pray a Scripture using your body position and posture to reenact what you read and feel.
- Dance to your favorite music.
- Make love with curiosity and playfulness.
- Slather your body with a special lotion or fragrance.
- Change your bedsheets and wear your favorite scent to sleep.

Conclude the day at bedtime by offering a blessing to God for each of your senses and your physical self.

Day 18: Tending to Others

This is my commandment, that you love one another as I have loved you. No one has greater love than this, to lay down one's life for one's friends. You are my friends if you do what I command you. I do not call you servants any longer, because the servant does not know what the master is doing; but I have called you friends, because I have made known to you everything that I have heard from my Father. You did not choose me but I chose you. And I appointed you to go and bear fruit, fruit that will last, so that the Father will give you whatever you ask him in my name. I am giving you these commands so that you may love one another. (John 15:12–17)

We are blessed to be able to tend to others in our life whom we know as our friends, lovers, relatives, coworkers, mentors, enemies, heroes, strangers or pets. We attach a quality of personal energy to every relationship. We can be energized, remain neutral or be drained by our interactions with various people. Tending to the quality of energy we have when we spend time with others offers us clues for making further decisions.

Some of our relationships are incredibly enriching, and in them we encounter a generative quality of energy and enthusiasm through our interactions. We actually experience increased vitality, and it is often mutual. These are the people with whom we resonate well and look forward to spending time with. Jesus was a person who generated positive energy. And because we know he loved people, especially his disciples and those who were marginalized, in all likelihood Jesus was rejuvenated and motivated by many of the people he spent his time with.

Other relationships are neutral for us. We are neither energized nor drained. We may genuinely enjoy the company or friendship of someone, but a deep life-giving dimension for ourselves and for the other is most likely not present.

Finally, there are those others that deplete energy from us. When we spend time with a person or organization that drains our vitality, the result is fatigue, frustration and even resentment. A sense of inner relief occurs when our interaction is concluded. Conversations are often spent in criticism and complaint. Our inner experience is very different depending upon our interaction with a person who creates synergy, is neutral to our energy or is exhausting.

Tending to others requires discernment in order to understand what value and building of the kingdom of God actually transpires. We need to spend more time in relationships of vitality, a smaller portion of time in neutral relationships, and begin to limit the people and situations that deplete our life force. This is certainly easier said than done and may at first appear to be harsh and selfish. But it is truly necessary. It is not meant to diminish the power of transformation that can occur during difficult interactions with others. Rather, it is about honoring personal limits of time and energy, and tending to the most important things with vigor and personal passionate presence. We discover inner peace and generosity increases when we are deliberate with our commitments and interactions with others.

MEDITATION

Breathe quietly for two minutes.

Reflect upon the various relationships with others in your life. In your journal quickly list the names of twenty-four people in your life. After you have made a list, go back and title the energy you experience with them in one of three ways— vitalizing, neutral or draining—based upon the majority of your interactions.

Rest in God's presence for two minutes.

In your journal write for fifteen minutes about what you wrote in your list. Are there any changes you want or need to make as you tend to the others in your life? Make note of your insights.

In your own manner, ask the Holy Spirit to empower your connection with others.

Day 19: Tending Burdens and Demands

> Come to me, all you that are weary and are carrying heavy
> burdens, and I will give you rest. Take my yoke upon you,
> and learn from me; for I am gentle and humble in heart,
> and you will find rest for your souls. For my yoke is easy,
> and my burden is light. (Matthew 11:28–30)

Jesus invites all who are burdened to find rest with him. All of us have burdens at various times throughout the hours and months of our life. Jesus knows each person carries individual burdens. The burdens and demands of our life are experienced differently from those of our neighbor or sibling because each human person is distinct. Jesus was right to invite us to turn to him for comfort and companionship, the same way we also turn to a close friend or community to experience support and a place to be heard and understood.

Tending to our burdens can be challenging. We may perceive that a burden or demand is a curse and miss the blessing buried beneath the surface. For one person a burden could be an illness, and for another a burden could be concern for a child, friend or parent. Burdens are personal, communal and global. Burdens and demands arrive in all forms and sizes ranging from disease to a lack of meaning in work to abuse or impoverishment. These burdens and demands originate from within the complexity of our own self or from external forces. The things and situations that continue to poke and prod at us are trying to get our attention so that we may discover a protected fruit of delight or deadly poison of harm and even sin.

Because life adjusts and transforms, what was once a gift or blessing can disintegrate to a burden or demand. Likewise, an original burden can transform into a blessing and grace. The value of tending to burdens is that they reveal a potential path of action. One young man discovered he was drawn into service for others and burdened by unease when he imagined following a prescribed male journey in an affluent country. Another woman praying and making a daily examination of conscience discovered that her self-righteous judgment of a sibling had become subtly abusive and toxic. A couple came to the understanding that a second house originally purchased as an investment and for weekend pleasure had gradually limited family choices of time and financial resources. You will have burdens specific to your own life.

We tend to burdens with accuracy and compassion just as in the garden we identify and pull weeds, careful to not disturb roots of healthy plantings nearby. Courage is essential, along with a small amount of trepidation sprinkled with humility. We very well may discover a need to change our inner perspective, external stance or significant commitment. Burdens will pop up waiting to be noticed, prayed with and transformed.

Humbleness of heart and Jesus help cultivate the path for us.

MEDITATION

Gather eight to ten rocks and a permanent marker. Choose a quiet place where you will not be interrupted. Spread the rocks around you. Sit quietly for two or more minutes centering in the present moment and God's holy presence.

Pick up a rock and hold it in your hands, allowing it to represent a burden in your life. Name the burden aloud and write a word on the rock representing your burden. Continue with as many rocks as you need. Place the rocks in a pile in front of you.

Simply breathe, gazing at rocks representing your burdens and demands.

If you are drawn to a particular rock, pick it up and begin an internal conversation with the circumstance the rock represents for you. Record in your journal and express the emotions and insight you receive. Tend to each rock with as much time as you need.

Gather all the rocks into your hands. Are you willing to ask Jesus to help you tend to your burdens? Can you let go of what no longer serves the spiritual garden of your deepest integrity?

PRAYER

> Dear Jesus,
> We seek to please you in so many ways that become distorted and full of harm and pain for others and ourselves.
>
> Permit me to understand your deepest truth for my life and that your desire for pruning and weeding is a vital, healthy action.
>
> Allow me to comprehend how burdens rob me of life and harden my spirit.

Teach me to turn to you for comfort and understanding when life seems too harsh to bear.

Guide me to bravery in the face of adversity and to a discovery of immense inner simplicity.

Release thought patterns and behaviors that stunt my life-giving passion and energy.

Draw me toward your wisdom of reverence, wonder, hope and potential, even in the face of my desolation and despair.

Bring your comfort to me now as I name the burden of (name words on each rock).

I entrust my life to your gentle and humble heart.

With gratitude I praise you, and ask for your blessing that the yoke of these rocks may be lifted, and I may be made anew. Amen.

Day 20: Tending the Still, Small Voice Within

Let anyone with ears to hear listen! (Mark 4:23)

God shares truth and love with the world in ongoing revelation. Beauty exists in the quiet heartbeat of the beloved. We learn to stop and attune our soul to listen, to be watered in the presence of God. Likewise, we tend to the small voice within our own heartbeat.

The truth God speaks gets buried by our layers of expectation, opinion and unfocused action. The grounding of our life can be likened to parched land, fertile soil or a watered garden. Our ability to listen with ears that hear is dependent upon the quality of our availability to the present moment. If our life resembles a watered garden, we are able to discern the still, small voice with clarity and vision. Fertile soil offers recognition. An inner life similar to parched land results in truth and love that is unacknowledged and useless.

Tending the garden of our soul requires effort and stillness. Cultivating positive emotion and thought allows an authentic part of self to be acknowledged and reverenced. Creating a safe place to listen to our own inner voice unobstructed from critique is the first step. Negative thought patterns and addictive behavior thwart the effort to listen deeply to God and our own inner truth. Unhealed wounds, sin and painful loss have potential to become lumps of stubborn clay. Our still, small voice easily goes into hiding.

To be heard, the inner voice of our wisdom requires a daily shower of stillness and prayer. In addition, awakened senses are needed, as is a deep trust of God's love and enduring goodness. Trusting and reverencing the still, small voice of inner truth is precious to God, others and us.

MEDITATION

Today will be spent constructing a safe inner space to tend to the still, small voice within.

Begin in stillness, focusing upon the feel of breath in your body. With your inhalation breath say the word *trust* to yourself. With your exhalation breathe out with the word *stillnesss* to yourself. Continue for five minutes.

You now have an occasion to design your own sacred inner sanctuary that you can visit any time. Enter into this meditation with your imagination and all of your senses awakened.

You are by yourself. Visualize a landscape or a structure of your choice. What do you see? Hear? Sense? Discover? This place is anything you desire. It is completely yours. Design your sacred sanctuary in any way you choose. What colors do you notice? Is it light or dark? Indoors or out? Where are you geographically? What sounds do you hear? Are there any aromas? Complete the vision of your inner temple and rest in your creation. You await an important visitor.

Be still. Look around and notice someone approaching you. You recognize the figure of Jesus. He approaches silently, smiling, looking into your eyes with care. You hear him asking if he may join you. You reply "yes." The two of you look at each other with love. He has come to listen to you. Begin sharing your heart in conversation to him with the still, small voice within you. What do you say first?

Take however long you need. He listens intently. Then listen to his response to you. Stay with him until you finish talking. Be still in his presence. Gradually become aware of when it is time to go. Jesus rises to say good-bye to you and embraces you. Hear him say to you, "I am with you always, I love you." Thank him for the time you've shared and watch him depart. Notice once again your surroundings. Offer thanksgiving to God. Look around again. You'll be back soon.

Slowly tend to present time, here and now. Wiggle your hands and toes. Breathe deeply. Take a moment to write in your journal about the inner sacred space you created. Consider that you can design multiple inner sanctuaries and visit for a quick moment or stay as long as you like, anytime.

Conclude with a favorite prayer of your own.

Day 21: Tending the Garden

Place yourself deliberately in God's presence and breathe quietly, stilling your mind.

Take your gardening tool and seed packet and place them in your hands.

Slowly pray Luke 13:6–9, the Scripture that began your week of tending the garden of your life.

Slowly review your week. Reflect upon your journal entries and daily reflections about where you experience delight and disappointment. Ask yourself the following questions reflecting upon your life as it has been lived in the details of this week:

- Where am I tending to God in my daily life? Am I challenged in any way?
- As I tend the garden of my life, what am I noticing?
- Are there areas I have identified that need more attention?
- Are there any weeds popping up that need to be pulled?
- Am I able to recognize the presence of God more readily?
- Has something new been planted in me this week?
- What type of garden does my life evoke in me this week?

Look closely at your gardening tool and seed packet. How do they speak to you symbolically about a week of tending to everyday details?

Record in your journal any insights, thoughts or feelings you experience.

Engage in some type of physical activity today that will stretch your body so you can appreciate the physical aspects of being alive!

Conclude by considering that your soul is a garden and that God enjoys daily walks with you.

Note: Begin making arrangements to plan for an entire play day for yourself in the fifth week of your retreat. This means that none of your usual activities will occur that day. This is an important part of the retreat, so please plan ahead. If you need to reframe your understanding of the day, think of it as a "mental-health day" for your soul! Please make arrangements for this opportunity. Plan the week to fit your schedule. If you need the day to be other than when it is designed in the retreat week, swap it. Just don't miss it! It takes effort to clear your schedule for the day, but please give this gift of a day to yourself!

WEEK FOUR: PRUNING AND APPRECIATING

Sometimes put yourself very simply before God, certain of his presence everywhere, and without any effort, whisper very softly to his sacred heart whatever your own heart prompts you to say.[1]

—Jane Francis de Chantal

I am the true vine, and my Father is the vinegrower. He removes every branch in me that bears no fruit. Every branch that bears fruit he prunes to make it bear more fruit. You have already been cleansed by the word that I have spoken to you. Abide in me as I abide in you. Just as the branch cannot bear fruit by itself unless it abides in the vine, neither can you unless you abide in me. I am the vine, you are the branches. Those who abide in me and I in them bear much fruit, because apart from me you can do nothing. Whoever does not abide in me is thrown away like a branch and withers; such branches are gathered, thrown into the fire, and burned. If you abide in me, and my words abide in you, ask for whatever you wish, and it will be done for you. My Father is glorified by this, that you bear much fruit and become my disciples. (John 15:1–8)

In any garden design it is necessary to make choices to allow some plants to grow and others to be pruned or even plucked from the earth. In a row of vegetables or flower seedlings, the gardener often plants duplicate seeds, understanding the time will come to thin new sprouts leaving healthy space for other seedlings to develop. As plants grow toward full maturity, they multiply and even will lean in the direction of one another. Inevitably a volunteer plant sprouts in an empty spot of soil. I prefer my gardens lush and full, and I often overplant. Invariably the time arrives when I must transplant a clump of lilies or penstemon that crowd their neighbors.

Our lives may resemble the same pattern. Through our senses, we engage so much beauty and goodness in the world that we want it all—we desire to experience as much life as possible. Perhaps this comes from the inherent knowledge that life itself is transitory, and in the grand scheme of things, short-lived on this planet. Nature is our steady reminder, and it also teaches that everything has a cycle and season. In our life seasons we enter stages where we learn, desire, collect, accumulate, appreciate, prune, simplify and give away. The spiritual discipline of fasting, in company with appreciation and simplification, helps clarify spiritual meaning in our everyday life and helps us to know what matters most to us.

Nothing is omitted from the spiritual realm of awareness. Every idea, person and thing that enters into our life is included in the arena of our potential consciousness. Therefore, our lives can swiftly grow very full. To live a whole, thus holy, life is first about living with a grateful heart. Following closely is an appreciation and praise of our creaturehood and interrelatedness with the rest of God's creation. Appreciation flows from our being in harmony with our life mission and the will of the Divine. Recognition of our calling, or in other words, our deepest conversation and interaction in the world, reveals what is lasting and real. Attentiveness to inner and outer life simplification offers opportunity for pruning and letting go of what no longer serves our neighbor or us. Real spiritual growth is made possible.

This week of your retreat will revolve around your increased ability to notice, appreciate and simplify. Your time will be spent reflecting upon the blessings and support in your life, sorrows you have experienced and granting God permission to help prune that which will never bear fruit within you. The spiritual practice of fasting is introduced, a discipline that purifies and creates occasions for deliberate feasting and praise. You will delight in the beauty and mystery of who you are. Finally, you will increase your desire for God in your life.

PEONY

The peony growing just outside my kitchen door is now nine inches tall with multiple thick stems continuing to form. I have the luxury of appreciating her plumped buds that barely swell, revealing petals sheltered tight. Stems lengthen and strengthen with help from a circular wired support. I notice multiple side buds and know that if Peony is to grow softball-sized blooms, it will be necessary to prune the smaller side flowers to leave energy for the first and larger blossoms. Every year it is painful to cut a potential flower, but it is necessary for the overall health of her growing cycle. So with clippers in hand, I carefully distinguish primary stalks and buds, and snip the side blossoms. A few weeds are beginning to grow in the soil nearby, and so I pull those too. In removing side blossoms and weeds, Peony has been given energy to pulse life toward her fullness of bloom and ultimate gift. Ants have begun to crawl busily toward her tender blooms, simply delighting in the sweet sap she provides. Praise is offered for her presence in the garden.

Day 22: Appreciating Myself

I will greatly rejoice in the LORD,
    my whole being shall exult in my God;
for he has clothed me with the garments of salvation,
    he has covered me with the robe of righteousness,
as a bridegroom decks himself with a garland,

and as a bride adorns herself with her jewels.
For as the earth brings forth its shoots,
and as a garden causes what is sown in it to spring up,
so the Lord GOD will cause righteousness and praise
to spring up before all the nations. (Isaiah 61:10–11)

The person you are today has been cultivated in part by time and action. Some life experiences have been of your own choosing, others not. This reflection will be spent simply being present to the beauty and individuality within you. For many people the words "I am…" have notes of familiarity. In a western cultural context we often introduce ourselves beginning by speaking "I am" followed by a name and title or descriptor of our identity. "I am" also may conjure an image of God from our close reading of the Old Testament. In the New Testament Jesus understands his identity is rooted in God and refers to himself multiple times stating "I am" and describing himself as the "bread of life," "the light of the world," "gate for the sheep," "good shepherd," "God's son," "the way the truth and the life" and "the Alpha and Omega." We discover our primary identity when we praise God and recognize we are clothed in garments of salvation. We learn to appreciate who we are through our profound relationship with God.

Gifts, talents and dreams rise from our experience, longing and relationship with self, God and others. In addition to natural abilities, there is within us and every person, something mysterious that attunes to certain places, people and activities that delight the deepest "I am." They are frequently evoked by the environment in which one lives. Some playful examples include a preference for dogs more than cats, mountains over the coastal region or plains, coffee instead of tea, the color purple more than green. Possibly a team sport is preferred in contrast to individual activities, and quiet solitary prayer is favored over active, communal prayer. Maybe you are comfortable with uncertainty and spontaneity, or you prefer structure and closure. Every person has a complex personality that includes emotion, thought and how the world is experienced through the senses. What we love and desire shapes our identity—our very own "I am" that rejoices in the Lord.

MEDITATION

Today is simple, yet challenging! You are to appreciate who you are in the life you are living, without censorship or critical thought, using one hundred percent of your senses. Throughout the next twenty-four hours, allow the following ideas to evoke attentiveness to your "I am" in your own skin.

- How do you appreciate the environment and people you encounter?
- Notice the way you look, act, feel and think. What captures your attention?
- Utilizing the gift of vision, allow your eyes to view the world around you with appreciation. Who are the people you engage with?
- With the gift of sound, listen to your voice in conversation with others and how it speaks within your own mind and heart. What words and sounds heard and unheard capture your attention?
- What smells attract? Repel? Are there tastes that you enjoy? Flavors you crave? What textures and energies do you feel?
- Who and what person or situation moves your heart to sorrow, empathy or appreciation?
- How does your mind engage with your efforts throughout the morning, afternoon and evening? Welcome your intuitive sense and pay attention to how it allows you to process information and respond to others.

- Finally, notice your breathing. Is it deep, shallow, almost nonexistent? Are there times you forget to breathe? Why? Return to your breath over and over throughout the day.

Carry a three-inch by five-inch card with you today. It is small enough to fit in a pocket, purse or wallet. Stop every hour of your waking day and just breathe for one minute. Ask yourself: What am I noticing? Are there particular things I appreciate about myself today? Write a one-line response on your card. At the end of the day review your reflections from the card.

PRAYER

Dear Holy One, Mysterious Creator of the Universe,
you delight and inspire me in countless ways.

Teach me to live each day as if the most important thing I
can do is to show up for the only life I've been given to live,
my own.

Allow me to appreciate the mystery of who you dream
me to be.

Show me how I am clothed in the garments of salvation
and turn my heart and vision to appreciate and desire your
will before all else.

Guide me to discover the beautiful person I am in you.

Take away anything in me that ceases to serve your good-
ness and love.

Please give me the sense to experience myself with your
gaze of holy love.

Lastly, I praise and thank you for this day in all of its
fragility and beauty.
Amen.

Day 23: Appreciating Blooms

For I am about to create new heavens
  and a new earth;

the former things shall not be remembered
  or come to mind.
But be glad and rejoice forever
  in what I am creating;
for I am about to create Jerusalem as a joy,
  and its people as a delight. (Isaiah 65:17–18)

A gardener sees with discerning eyes of love and appreciation. In the early morning or at dusk, a gardener walks quietly outdoors, pausing with wonder and appreciation before growing plants, flowers, berries, trees. Perhaps while watering, the gardener notices a plant that needs a little extra care, where a new bud has formed, or how a blossom is reaching fullness. The gardener may stand still and breathe—offering carbon dioxide as gift to the plants. Be present to what is alive in the moment, no longer thinking of the labor of the past or any future use or purpose. Personally, passionately be present in the moment of now. With all senses awakened, attend to only just this, just this— right now. Time passes swiftly when one is completely present in the here and now of life. An experience of interwoven connectedness can be realized. A feeling of spontaneous gratitude might well up within the human heart.

The purpose of this retreat is for you to recognize the spirituality of your everyday life and tend to God's presence already walking with you. Every day we are created anew. Hopefully the past twenty-two days have increased the awareness of your spiritual self and led you into more conscious, deliberate engagement with God through moments and minutes. From a spiritual perspective, classical terms for this process are described as: living with a discerning heart, mindfulness practice or taking a long, loving look at the really real. To develop a discerning heart is to listen for the subtle stirrings of the Holy Spirit, which guide us in understanding what is most valuable in any given situation. The spiritual person seeks to know God's will and more than anything else wants to bring God's love into the world through a union that leads to action, deed and service.

To cultivate union with God in the garden of details and daily life, deliberate prayer practices are necessary. Today you will review some of the blooms that prayer brings.

MEDITATION

Begin in stillness, focusing upon the feel of breath in your body. With your inhalation, breathe in saying the word *gentle* to yourself. With your exhalation, breathe out the word *peace* to yourself. Continue until your attention is fully present.

Write in your journal or draw an image that represents what blooms for you in:

- your regular prayer practice,
- the image of God you like best,
- an experience of religion or church,
- during a time of decision,
- a significant relationship,
- past prayer experience.

Conclude by reviewing how you expressed yourself. Choose one image or word to take forward into the remainder of your day. Offer a spontaneous prayer from your heart to God.

Day 24: Pruning Side Blossoms

Either make the tree good, and its fruit good; or make the tree bad, and its fruit bad; for the tree is known by its fruit. (Matthew 12:33)

As flowers grow, multiple blossoms may be present on one stem. Tree branches originate from a main trunk. Vines send multiple tendrils from their stalk. Bromeliads and select tropical plants *pup*. Aspen trees grow *suckers*. If you've ever grown basil, a rose bush or almost any other plant, you know that you must pinch or prune some side growth in order to allow primary energy to surge forth and create a vital healthy plant. What at first appears to be a sacrifice actually benefits the plant and creates vitality. The same is true in our spiritual garden.

When we delight in growth, it is challenging to deliberately remove beauty that will subtly divert energy. It is much easier to remove visibly unhealthy stems or limbs or to extract nearby weeds.

A discerning, reflective presence is necessary if we want to live with an atmosphere of fullness and abundance for ourselves and the world at large. To know our strengths and how the world needs us and then to act according to that knowledge is blessed. Beyond the question: "Is this the best thing I can do in this moment of time?" must be: "Is this necessary?" The virtue of fasting prepares us to discern the difference between what is truly needed and what is merely "fluff." In all honesty, not much time is really available for us to really live the life we dream and that God dreams within us. That is why it is so important to fast from mediocrity and choose carefully where our attention is focused and given away. Some trees and plants have longer life spans than humans do!

When appreciating the side blossoms of inner growth and visible manifestations of a life in the Spirit, we learn to listen more alertly to our inner rhythms and moods. Your inner self knows truth—more than you suspect—and will reveal the guidance you need to help you flow in deep streams of living water. Your body knows the sensation of grace and joy and remembers on a cellular level. So too, your body knows the feeling of trauma, alienation and sin. Perhaps that is why some of the sexual sins that are physically experienced seem to acquire much greater notice than other equally important sins such as glut-tony, abuse of power and social injustice.

The deliberate discipline of fasting reveals what is real and offers an appreciation of how little we truly need. The art of fast-ing creates spaciousness for a greater dependence on God and room for the Holy Spirit to move into our soul and relationships. A fast is not limited to a food source we no longer ingest into our bodies. The choice to fast from harsh language, self-criticism, judgment of others, busyness or unimportant distractions can open a space within us for a greater capacity to love. When we attend to the seven deadly sins of pride, envy, anger, sloth, greed, gluttony and lust through fasting and pruning, we acquire purity and a deeper appreciation for God and things of the world.

MEDITATION

Sit still for one minute and focus on your breathing.

Imagine yourself as a blooming plant or tree. What image immediately comes to mind? In your journal or on a separate piece of paper, employ markers, crayons or paints and draw to the best of your ability a botanical representation of the image you chose. No one will see this but you. When you finish, use a pen to name all the different parts of your life represented by the drawing.

Choose one area in your life where beautiful growth is occurring, but something seems to be sapping energy from your potential. Look at what clutters. It could be a thought pattern, emotion, alienating behavior, person or situation that has become a limitation to you. From what you have identified, choose one thing you want to intentionally fast from in the next twenty-four hours. Your choice can be as simple as a tone of voice, spending money, self-doubt, critical thoughts or disillu-sionment. Whatever you choose, be deliberate. This is something that prevents you from bringing love in the world and experiencing inner serenity.

Throughout the day allow the beauty of the plant or tree you envisioned to replace your mood. Be gentle with yourself. You are a mystery unfolding.

Conclude the day by praying a favorite prayer slowly and deliberately.

Day 25: Pruning the Unnecessary

In the same way, my friends, you have died to the law through the body of Christ, so that you may belong to another, to him who has been raised from the dead in order that we may bear fruit for God. While we were living in the flesh, our sinful passions, aroused by the law, were at work in our members to bear fruit for death. But now we are discharged from the law, dead to that which held us captive, so that we are slaves not under the old written code but in the new life of the Spirit. (Romans 7:4–6)

Through fasting, a person's perception of the world expands, offering greater awareness of value and meaning. One year I refrained from consuming sugar and flour for health purposes. After a few weeks it wasn't difficult. One Sunday at a Catholic Mass, I had a profound experience. At the church I attended the eucharistic bread was homemade by parishioners in contrast to paper-thin wafers used in many Catholic churches in the United States. On that Sunday, as I received the Body of Christ and placed the host in my mouth, sensation exploded like never before. The fullness of flavor in whole wheat bread was exquisite! Sensation, texture, taste, scent and awareness flooded my soul truly transforming the Eucharist into a sensual, life-offering force within me. I returned to my place in the pew stunned with new appreciation that THIS was the intensity with which Christ wants to come into my life, to us all. It was a transforming moment as I gazed at the faces in the community gathered to worship God, love one another and go into the world to love and heal. Fasting from sugar and flour had opened me to a profound experience of love. It may have been an accidental side effect, but God makes use of every opportunity to break open our understanding so that we can receive love more deeply and then give it away.

There are many ways to fast. Throughout the past weeks you have experienced fasting in your own way and by your choice to enter into this retreat. Fasting allows you to grow toward an aspiration and enter into solidarity with others. Many Christians I have worked with over the past eighteen years tend to limit fasting to a food, or obvious sinful behavior, correlating fasting to purification. While that remains an important understanding of fasting, it is not the only one. Your actions and thoughts create illusions and cause alienation from others and from God. Fasting breaks open our understanding of connectedness. Your fasting is not just personal; it affects the whole body of Christ.

The concept of fasting from socially accepted norms requires a different vision and mindset from fasting from food or sin. It means taking a clear, firm look at your life and determining what appears to bring goodness to your life but actually bleeds energy from your core purpose. This occurs in many ways. Some examples include:

- You volunteer in the community (outside the home), and your attention and time is compromised so much that you are not there for a child or family member in need.
- You place a large emphasis on acquiring a beautiful house and material possessions, while neglecting the people

who live in the home and neighborhood.

- Your children and teens are involved in too many extracurricular activities, and consequently you all have very little time together.
- You purchase items that may have harmed another person or even the environment during production.
- You remain in a work environment that is unethical and without principles.
- You spend an inordinate amount of time on the Internet, watching television, working or shopping.

These are only a few examples of actions negatively impacting your core identity in socially acceptable ways. To effectively prune away the actions that are not needed, you must become still enough to distinguish what brings your joy, creativity and passion alive. The gift from the process of simplification and pruning is a new appreciation for what you did not know you already knew, spaciousness for the not-yet-discovered and increased energy to focus upon your core values and what is truly important: the life God desires you live.

MEDITATION

Breathe gently for five minutes, paying attention to where your mind and heart wander.

You will go for three different walks during your meditation time. The first will be through your home, the second with your commitments and the third with your inner heart. Invite God to partner with you as you enter into your reflection. Ask to perceive with fresh eyes and insight and to be open to whatever becomes apparent.

Begin by taking an actual physical walk through your home. Cross the threshold of the front door as if it were the first time you had ever entered your home. Walk through each room slowly and intently. What do you notice? Open closets, drawers, windows. What does your home reveal about your life?

Take a symbolic walk through your daily life commitments and those of any children or others who depend upon you. What transpires?

Go for a long walk outdoors, alone. Allow thoughts and images from your own personal inner experience to enter your mind as you put one foot in front of the next. What comes to light?

Conclude with reflection to determine what no longer serves your life and ability to be present and love. Decide to give it away. Let it go. God knows what to do with anything you let go of and is with you in the process and beyond. End with a favorite prayer.

Day 26: Appreciating Sorrows

Surely goodness and mercy shall follow me
  all the days of my life,
and I shall dwell in the house of the LORD
  my whole life long. (Psalm 23:6)

The discovery of a deep wound can become a transformative gift or a wrenching sorrow that opens the heart and soul to longing and realized grace, which is at the core of Christian mystery. No matter who we are, at some time in our life we experience sorrow. We have a choice to either become bitter or become hopeful. Suffering hallows us and invites us to connect with God and others to receive support and care. Sorrow can teach empathy and expand our notion of reality and the world we live in. The potential for spiritual growth in our sorrow and brokenness is found in the detection that it is possible to experience gratitude or even appreciation for what once may have been unbearable.

How can the plant world inform human life about suffering? Deforestation and poisoning from chemicals and pesticides are two ways. Another is simply neglect and lack of appreciation by world inhabitants. Though this isn't suffering in the classical sense, it can reveal the interrelatedness of earth and humans and inspire reverence for the lands that feed, nourish, clothe and sustain humankind.

Years ago I was able to learn a spiritual lesson from some plants at a garden center. During the summer months I worked at a family-owned nursery creating hanging moss baskets and caring for plants and customers. A small section was reserved for ailing plants and was designated "the hospital." Every day during my morning watering rounds, I walked through rows of plants struggling to thrive. They ranged in size from two-inch starters to large boxed trees. I paid careful attention to why each plant was there and what I needed to give to each plant to help it thrive. Was this particular plant drooping from oversaturation of water, or shriveled from not enough water? Had I placed a shade-loving plant in the sun? Was a bug or fungus attaching itself to leaves or roots? Every plant required specific attention. One day I decided to dose the plants in need of help with my fertilizer of choice: fish emulsion.

It's hard to match the pungent smell and thick, goopy consistency of pure fish emulsion composed of fish by-product, menhaden fish and a few unknowns. In other words, it's not a very pleasant fertilizer to work with. In order to distribute the fertilizer I had to dilute the fish-puree in water and fill two large watering cans. Trip after trip, I mixed, carried and applied. At the end of an hour, the wet mixture was on my sandaled feet, shorts and was even dripping down my arms. Neighborhood cats had come to visit, drawn by the smell. In the end, the plants had what they needed to thrive—and I needed a long hot shower!

Within days, the stinky, repulsive, rotten mixture had begun its magic. Little two-inch perennials looked a bit greener. Yellowed ferns showed color moving through their fronds. Herbs stood a little stronger. What had seemed utterly repulsive to me had been life-giving to the plants. Gradually most of them returned to the nursery stock, healthier from their experience. I have continued to fertilize using fish emulsion in my own garden, having learned its good purpose.

In a loose analogy, suffering fertilizes us in a similar way as fish emulsion does for a plant. What is stinky and repulsive at the time can also hold life-giving spiritual potential. We do not need to go out of our way looking for suffering. Just living daily life will bring challenge, pain and loss without any choice on our part. On a side note, it is important not to be misled into believing that God causes suffering deliberately to punish, from vengeance or because it might be good for us. That is not the nature of God revealed by Jesus. Free will and the nature by which we live (with death) allows suffering to occur. God is already waiting for us with comfort and consolation in every painful situation. What we can do is choose our response. Knowing there are psychological steps in the grieving process can be helpful. A glimmer of hope in the face of suffering is the spiritual gift, offering new meaning and purpose for our lives. Stinky and repulsive, most often unasked for and unwanted, the gift of suffering brings new life and spiritual growth to our garden.

MEDITATION

Find a quiet place outdoors to sit and be still. Pay attention to your breathing. When you are still and centered in God, reflect upon how some type of suffering in your life has become a blessing of sorts in the present time. How did the shift in your understanding occur?

Next, if it feels safe to you, allow a present anguish to come to mind. Settle your attention upon how a shift in your awareness and understanding might occur using the fish emulsion story and your own past experience.

End with a spontaneous prayer of thanksgiving in your own words or by praying Psalm 23 (The Lord Is My Shepherd).

Day 27: Appreciating Support

Our steps are made firm by the LORD,
    when he delights in our way;
though we stumble, we shall not fall headlong,
    for the LORD holds us by the hand. (Psalm 37:23–24)

In the first half of life we need boundaries, limits and people that provide structure for us. In the second half of life we move beyond dualisms into varying complexities of understanding the world around us. From a spiritual and developmental perspective, the relationships and support we need from institutions, people, belief systems and even ourselves begin to shift. This is good and necessary for our spiritual growth, and we need companions that can help us in our journey.[2]

In a garden various plants and vines also need support in their growth cycle. The gardener provides staking, poles, trellis, fencing, banding and more to help the plants thrive. In our life various people enter, remain and exit both at ordinary and critical times. We encounter family members, friends, strangers and organizations that help support us. They will challenge, uphold, encourage and suffer with us in seen and unseen ways. Because of them we experience God's love and a sense of community with one another. Supportive people invite us to become our best selves. When someone really listens to us and we see the essence of our goodness reflected in his or her face, we receive a gift. The best support people become soul companions.

A soul companion is a safe person who loves you uncondi-
tionally and puts flesh on God for you, offering you the dignity
of your personhood. Perhaps a spouse or partner, friend, family
member, coworker or member of a religious community is your
soul companion. There are no limits to define who can be a soul
companion. Ideally you already know through personal experience that God is your soul companion. Saints and people who
have gone before you can be mystical companions. You never
need to hide from an affirming and supportive soul friend. No
mask or show of our false self is necessary. The soul friend provides a mirror for you to use to reflect back the genuine goodness and truth you have such a hard time seeing in yourself.

MEDITATION

Today will be spent appreciating the supportive people, places
and structures in your life. It is a time to celebrate the unity of
human purpose and to love one another.

Go for a walk.

Reflect upon the people in your life who have supported
you, and who at times, like a vine, you may have clung to for
dear life. Who are the individuals or even four-legged creatures
that have been your soul friends? Allow your memories to move
your heart to appreciation and praise.

When you return from your walk, write a note or call one
person who came to mind during this reflection. Let her know
the difference she made in your life.

PRAYER

> Spirit of Wisdom,
>> This day I offer you my appreciation and gratitude.
>> Your mighty understanding of me gently brings support at
> exactly the appointed time.
>> Never have I been truly abandoned from your presence

revealed in creatures that befriend me in love and compan-
ionship.

No matter the hardship, show me the face of your love in
the structures and support of soul friends.

Allow me to appreciate the gift of others in time of distress
and joy.

Open my heart to your presence through the lives of
saints and holy companions.

Teach me to seek your love that I may know when to cling
and when to let go into the mystery of life growth.

Deepen supports that lead me toward interior freedom, as
I become the person you dream me to be.

Guide me to be a soul companion for others.

Thank you for the gifts of … (name people) in my life.

I place myself today and forever in your vital, loving, sup-
portive embrace.

Amen.

Day 28: Appreciating and Pruning

Place yourself deliberately in God's presence and breathe quietly, stilling your mind.

Take your gardening tool and seed packet and place them in
your hands.

Slowly pray John 15:1–8, the Scripture that began your week
of pruning and appreciating.

Today you will spend time reflecting about pruning and
appreciating. Slowly review your week. Reflect upon your journal
entries and daily reflections about where you experience delight
and disappointment. Ask yourself the following questions, reflecting upon your life as it has been revealed to you this week:

- Where am I encountering God in my daily life?
- Am I inspired in any way?
- How is my appreciation for my everyday life increasing?
- Am I aware of any aspects of my life in need of fasting or pruning?
- Has something been growing in me this week?
- What type of garden does my life evoke in me? Describe it.
- Look closely at your gardening tool and seed packet. How do they speak to you symbolically about a week of pruning and appreciation?

Record in your journal about any insights, thoughts or feelings you experience.

Conclude by whispering softly in prayer to God whatever your heart prompts you to share.

WEEK FIVE: GATHERING FRUITS

If God is the center of your life, no words will be needed.
Your mere presence will touch their hearts.[1]

—Vincent de Paul

My beloved speaks and says to me:
"Arise, my love, my fair one,
  and come away;
for now the winter is past,
  the rain is over and gone.
The flowers appear on the earth;
  the time of singing has come,
and the voice of the turtledove
  is heard in our land.
The fig tree puts forth its figs,
  and the vines are in blossom;
    they give forth fragrance.
Arise, my love, my fair one,
  and come away...." (Song of Solomon 2:10–13)

In the beginning was the word, and the word was with God. Through time the word of God seeds, grows, spreads and feeds the body, earth and soul with nourishment and divine life in the here and now, the ordinary everyday. The seed ripens and grows to its fullness in the original intent and mystery. Our lives are like this too. We reach a time when we understand, appreciate and integrate our sense of belonging to the life we have been given to live and the divine call that invites us to action. We learn we are the beloved and in a pleasurable relationship with our God. The glory of a person fully alive emanates a gorgeous, magnificent unfolding that, like the word in the beginning, feeds and nourishes.

A garden reveals growth and maturity in a shorter amount of time than we generally see in our own lives. Maturity is visually evident. A garden is a gateway into God's hope for our own lives—that we too can blossom into fullness of life. The presence of God draws us toward deeper life, toward meaning beyond ourselves. Like flowers stretching in the direction of light, we crave a relationship with the Divine. Whether we name it or not, our hearts long for God and are restless until we plant roots in God's will and passionate desire for us.

When a gardener recognizes that a fruit has ripened, a flower has unfurled, or a tree fully leafs, deep gladness arises within the soul and spills into expression with laughter and wonder. Fragrant flowers, pungent herbs, vital vegetables and juicy fruit all reveal one thing: a primary life force within all creation desiring fruition. At this time, only one thing is necessary from the gardener, a grace-filled gaze at just this: fullness of presence and intent attained. The response is simple: gratitude. Prayer is spontaneous; the work of gardening reveals results! And without our full, conscious, active participation, the ripening still occurs. The same thing happens in our spiritual garden. We show up for life and do our best. Opening our heart to prayer, God transforms us. We do not do it on our own. God is at work in our life. This week as you garden through daily reflections, you will embrace the beauty of who you are, which is far more powerful than you dream.

God dwells with humanity. We know this intellectually, but we do not fully know it spiritually. History shows us over and over again that we plainly do not believe in the power of love. If we did, Jesus would not have been crucified, famine and war would not continue to be worldwide occurrences, and abuse of every kind would cease. God keeps trying to help us get it right as we struggle to accept the truth of who we are: the beloved of a living God. We discount the power and potential of being agents of positive change and mercy in the world. Why do we think less of who we are than the Creator does?

The solitary rose, daisy, lacy columbine, pungent penstemon and blade of grass proclaim their reality—*this is it*. An example from the Gospel of Matthew teaches us not to worry, implying that we have to just live fully by placing our trust in God:

> Therefore I tell you, do not worry about your life, what you will eat or what you will drink, or about your body, what you will wear. Is not life more than food, and the body more than clothing? Look at the birds of the air; they neither sow nor reap nor gather into barns, and yet your heavenly Father feeds them. Are you not of more value than they? And can any of you by worrying add a single hour to your span of life? And why do you worry about clothing? Consider the lilies of the field, how they grow; they neither toil nor spin, yet I tell you, even Solomon in all his glory was not clothed like one of these. But if God so clothes the grass of the field, which is alive today and tomorrow is thrown into the oven, will he not much more clothe you—you of little faith? (Matthew 6:25–30)

What inside you is afraid to stand up and rejoice in the glory of who you are? Dare you delight in who you are? Can you agree to let your life reveal the magnificence of God who creates, redeems and dreams you into fullness of life? Jesus promised to bring you abundant life. Trust it is God's desire and will that you love and play in the flowering garden of your life.

Throughout this week you will be gathering details and awareness of the ordinary everyday, the delights and principles creating support and full bloom for you. You will gather a bouquet from the fruits of the Spirit shared with others through your actions and reflect upon the spiritual blossoming of forgiveness and reconciliation. Finally, you will identify how your heart hears a concern for the world that can become a flowering of great contribution for others. Be forewarned! On the third day of this week, you will need to clear your calendar and arrange for a day of play. If you need to substitute the order of the days, please do. Plan this week to work with your life. But please, don't skip the day designed for you to play and gather delight in your spiritual garden.

PEONY

Against the south wall of the house, Peony stretches in mid-morning sunlight, moving this way and that in the slight breeze. Buds have expanded and one begins to unfurl. Ruffled edges are a perfect pink. There is nothing to do for her now. The heavy rain, which fell the day before last, soaked her roots. I crouch on the step, and look closely. I ponder her presence. I wonder if I dare cut the stem to bring her indoors. Her invitation is to stop the busyness and sit still, in the open air. She will bloom longer if left on the stem where she grows. Her energy will go back into flowering next year if she is not cut. Responding to the invitation, I settle on a warm stone step and listen to a chorus of songbirds, the far-off drone of a plane, a buzzing bee nearby. The garden vibrates with life, awakened to the morning. Noticing delicate perfumes in the air, I examine ants crawling on her plump bud and stems. A tiny-winged bug lands upon a spring-green, veined leaf and flutters. Rabbit has left a gift of fertilizer pellets at her base. Peony reveals patience and purpose. Quiet breath and gratitude for her instruction of how to live remain. Revealing beauty, truth and God's glory, Peony is simply Peony. Can we show up for life in the same way?

Day 29: Gathering Fruit of the Ordinary

He also said, "With what can we compare the kingdom of God, or what parable will we use for it? It is like a mustard seed, which, when sown upon the ground, is the smallest of all the seeds on earth; yet when it is sown it grows up and becomes the greatest of all shrubs, and puts forth large branches, so that the birds of the air can make nests in its shade." (Mark 4:30–32)

Many of us grow up with the message that to be ordinary lacks value. The opposite is true in our spiritual journey. To be content with the ordinary is to be fully in tune with oneself. Holiness flows from the roots of the ordinary and humble. Nature reveals the complexity of this understanding to us. Jesus taught us to encounter riches in the ordinary events of the everyday: in a mustard seed, grain of wheat, pearl, lily of the field, while filling a water bucket, preparing a meal, washing feet. Jesus demonstrates how to cultivate a heart of wonder in our everyday, teaching us to see with new eyes.

The ordinary occurs in the midst of washing pots and pans, responding to a crying child, sitting in a board meeting or acknowledging a homeless woman on the street. It is in these moments that we can welcome God, patiently waiting for us. Bringing our full attention to the present moment is at the core of a spiritual life. Spirituality, resembling any great relationship, is not about the peak moments. Rather, the value is revealed in the day-in and day-out of living. Most often this occurs in details. If we cannot encounter God in the hours of our week, how do we expect to meet God on Sunday at church? Christians don't worship and interact with a God that is separate from the events of the world or their own daily life.

Gathering the ordinary teaches when enough is enough and allows our senses to be fed with simplicity. We view life with eyes of wonder and awe, and we care for one another with reverence. We discover how to be humble and simple of heart. Humility and ordinariness flow with rich spiritual wisdom.

MEDITATION

Quiet your breathing.

Imagine you are going for a walk in a spring meadow. Is it morning? Noon? Sunset? What do you see? Smell? Hear? Wander for a while and find a place to sit. Be still. Allow ordinary images of your life to come into your consciousness and speak to you and call you by name. Imagine the images beginning to bloom around you. Rest in the sunlight knowing you sit with God. Begin to ask yourself: Who are the people I encounter with regularity? What obligations and chores are for me alone? Are there things and actions I continue to put off for another day? What is most ordinary about my life? Do I embrace the ordinary with love in my heart? How do ordinary events bloom in my days? Sit and ponder: What has bloomed around me? Use your imagination to gather a bouquet of the ordinary in your life.

Write in your journal for ten minutes about any thoughts you want to gather and remember.

Conclude in your own words by offering a prayer of thanksgiving for the ordinary in your life. Slowly pray the Lord's Prayer with special attention to the words: *Give us this day our daily bread.*

Day 30: Gathering Fruit of the Spirit

By contrast, the fruit of the Spirit is love, joy, peace, patience, kindness, generosity, faithfulness, gentleness, and self-control. (Galatians 5:22–23a)

Before we can give love away, we must know we are loved. To share joy, we need to have the experience of joy and delight within our soul. For peace and patience to flower, we must be patient and accepting of others and ourselves. The unparalleled gift of kindness is nurtured by gentleness and generosity of thought and deed. Faithfulness comes from living our commitments with integrity. Finally, self-control grows from a profound daily relationship with God through the person of Jesus, fully human, fully divine.

A life sharing the fruits of the Spirit with the world is whole, holy and a healing balm. Within each of us are moments of peace, kindness, generosity, forgiveness and faithfulness. In order for our life to fully bloom with the graces of the Holy Spirit, we know that time must be spent in prayer, silence and communion with God. Thus, we develop a heart of surrender and become a vessel of blessing for others, especially the poor and outcast from society. When our soul rests in the Holy One though prayer and service, imperceptibly God transforms us. Perfection is not possible in this life, and it should not be the goal. Desire for God and surrender to God's Spirit are the goals providing the roots for deeply realized union with our Creator. From a stance of utter trust, surrender and faith in God's holy embrace, we flower and bear fruit; watered with grace, we grow with the Spirit. Our participation is required to attune the mind, body and heart to God. To our surprise, over time we become gentler, kinder, more forgiving. We reflect the compassion and love of God to the world, in our homes and communities. People will be drawn to discover what—and who—brings such light alive within us.

Sounds of splashing water interrupted my writing. Sitting on a dock, I looked toward the shoreline for the source. A robin was bathing at the lake's edge creating a delightful ruckus.

There she stood, twenty feet away, on a little rock, knee deep in water. Over and over Robin dipped her face into the lake, fluttered her wings, arched her head and then stood still. Perhaps fifteen times she repeated the ritual. Suddenly, moving to a rock just beyond the waters reach, she stopped still in the morning sun. One minute passed, then another. Not moving, I watched, breathing quietly. In an instant, she—or maybe it was a he—rose into flight, chirping and singing. With wings now extended, Robin flew five feet from me, just at eye height, following the shoreline. My awareness of all around me expanded as the singing of birds from the garden a hundred yards from the shoreline grew in intensity. Robin took a dip, turned and flew to join her companions in the trees. I wondered: "How can Robin articulate the fruits of the Spirit to me, to you?" The answer was in her surrender to the joyful ritual of a bath, faithfulness of a morning splash, acknowledgment of sunshine, trust in flight, singing generously her song for this little corner of the world and building a nest in the garden. Robin had gathered her essence into fluid motion.

MEDITATION

Breathe quietly in God's presence. Slowly read Galatians 5:22–23a. In your journal list the fruits of the Spirit. Identify aspects of your life where each fruit of the Spirit is revealed though your life actions. Reflect upon how the fruits of the Spirit mature slowly and secretly in your life. Write in your journal about any insights you gather.

Conclude by slowly breathing in the meaning of the Scripture verse once again.

Day 31: Gathering Fruit of Delight

Praise the LORD!
Praise God in his sanctuary;

> praise him in his mighty firmament!
> Praise him for his mighty deeds;
> > praise him according to his surpassing greatness!
>
> Praise him with trumpet sound;
> > praise him with lute and harp!
> Praise him with tambourine and dance;
> > praise him with strings and pipe!
> Praise him with clanging cymbals;
> > praise him with loud clashing cymbals!
> Let everything that breathes praise the LORD!
> Praise the LORD! (Psalm 150)

Life is too short to miss out on playing and praising the Lord. Within all the hours we are given to live, a great spaciousness exists alongside our mortality. Grace-filled moments afford us the opportunity to experience life and share with one another. Still, we miss too many precious opportunities for an assortment of reasons, some good and several poor. We have many excuses for why we cannot avail ourselves of time to "play." We think of "play" as a luxury, time away from work we cannot afford to take. Perhaps we perceive leisure as an extravagance that we cannot accept within the confines and demands we set for ourselves and for which others hold us accountable. But spontaneity is a lovely bloom in the spiritual garden! The unexpected jolts us from mediocrity and refreshes us for new growth. Today is simple. You will show up for your life to play and be recreated!

To plan for your play day, review *Day 9: Seeds of Play*. How do you want to spend your day? Prepare your day of leisure ahead of time, and plan who, if anyone, you want to include. If you choose to have a companion during an outing, arrange to spend a minimum five-hour time block by yourself. The most important thing today is to choose carefully anything that will enrich your spirit. What do you really love to do? Do it! Go to a botanical garden, museum, concert, bookstore with coffee, out to lunch or read a great book. Plan for a hike and picnic, a visit to the plant nursery, play time in the garden or a favorite hobby or sport interest. Go to Mass, or visit a nearby monastery. If you normally awake early, sleep in. If you usually sleep in late, wake at dawn. Immerse your senses in the world and take delight in your life. It's your day to celebrate the gift of life.

Remember: PLAY all day!

MEDITATION

Conclude your day by reviewing the day with eyes of delight. Offer praise to God for the people you encountered, the emotions you experienced, the challenges you faced and the insights you gained. Decide if a day of leisure once a month might be valuable in your spiritual garden. If your answer is affirmative, choose a date for next month now!

PRAYER

> Come, bless the LORD, all you servants of the LORD,
>   who stand by night in the house of the LORD!
> Lift up your hands to the holy place,
>   and bless the LORD.
>
> May the LORD, maker of heaven and earth,
>   bless you from Zion. (Psalm 134)

Day 32: Gathering Fruit of Life Principles

My soul clings to you;
  your right hand upholds me. (Psalm 63:8)

In the garden of our soul, we have roots, supports and principles providing the foundation for our life of integrity. From a young age we experiment, learn guiding actions and principles. A baby's small hand will grasp a caregiver's extended finger and grip it securely. The garden vine covered in heavy blooms will tendril, entwining itself around support structures. As we age and mature, we learn to seek out support through relationships that offer us the ability to bloom into fullness. We become skilled at relying upon God and our own inner strength and potential. Gradually we come to understand our core beliefs and the foundational principles, which enable us to reach our life's full purpose. We discover that there are ethical, and often difficult, choices we must make, even when we don't desire to do so. Thoughts and actions become integrated. But when we are grounded in the gospel of truth and compassion, we become transparent to others.

The core principles we base our life upon influence actions every day. Jesus offers a prime example of how to model our life and determine what we are willing to live and die for. To begin with, Jesus had a profound relationship with his *Abba* that informed his thoughts and actions. Our primary guiding principles must also be founded with God the Creator through our relationship with Jesus and influence our daily choices. In addition to his relationship with his father, Jesus demonstrated commitment to his friends, mother and the seemingly invisible people existing on the margins of society. We too then are invited into enlivening relationships with family, friends and those people who are often forgotten and ignored.

The carpenter from Galilee also showed a phenomenal commitment to his faith community. He understood and lived his Jewish faith tradition and was knowledgeable of the Torah, known to Christians as the Old Testament. He knew the letter of the Jewish law inside out, and it did not prevent him from abiding by the law that his Father had written in his heart. Though Jesus understood and abided by Jewish law, Jesus also honored the dignity and mystery of every human person—and at times this got him into trouble. Jesus put God's people above the law—even the Jewish law. This is exactly why he was so countercultural, in his time and today. Modeling Jesus, we are commanded to know, internalize and articulate our faith tradition, then act with mercy and compassion in the world. Finally the humble God-man from Nazareth knew the values and principles he ascribed to in daily life. He uttered them beautifully through the Beatitudes recorded in Scripture and in his daily actions with Jews and gentiles alike.

When we align our values and principles with those of Jesus, we can expect to eventually experience misunderstanding, alienation and persecution in our place of work, faith community and even in family life. We may encounter personal or political rejection by organizations or friends. Nevertheless, the utmost importance remains to know and understand our values and to love with integrity. Even when no one is watching! What are the principles that keep you rooted and allow your life to flower and reach fruition? Do you cling to certain values and relationships that support and offer guidance to your life?

MEDITATION

Breathe quietly for five minutes, gathering your mind, heart and body to stillness.

In your journal, number a list from one to ten. Identify ten core principles or primary relationships you cling to and live by. Some words to get you started could include:

I commit to _____

I value _____

These people _____

My life _____

I cling to _____

The structure of _____

My parents taught me _____

When I was a child I learned _____

As an adult I _____

Jesus shows me _____

God enlightens me to _____

When you complete your list, write the ten sentences on a piece of paper. Then place the principles you have gathered on your prayer table, in a wallet or purse, in a Bible or another place that you value. Let them remind you of the principles that allow your life to flower.

PRAYER

> *Blessed are the poor in spirit, for theirs is the kingdom of heaven.*
> *Blessed are those who mourn, for they will be comforted.*
> *Blessed are the meek, for they will inherit the earth.*
> *Blessed are those who hunger and thirst for righteousness, for they will be filled.*
> *Blessed are the merciful, for they will receive mercy.*
> *Blessed are the pure in heart, for they will see God.*
> *Blessed are the peacemakers, for they will be called children of God.*
> *Blessed are those who are persecuted for righteousness' sake, for theirs is the kingdom of heaven.*
> *Blessed are you when people revile you and persecute you and utter all kinds of evil against you falsely on my account.*
> *Rejoice and be glad, for your reward is great in heaven, for in the same way they persecuted the prophets who were before you. (Matthew 5:3–12)*

Day 33: Gathering Fruit of Forgiveness

As God's chosen ones, holy and beloved, clothe yourselves with compassion, kindness, humility, meekness, and patience. Bear with one another and, if anyone has a complaint against another, forgive each other; just as the Lord has forgiven you, so you also must forgive. Above all, clothe yourselves with love, which binds everything together in perfect harmony. And let the peace of Christ rule in your hearts, to which indeed you were called in the one body. And be thankful. (Colossians 3:12–15)

Forgiveness is one of the greatest gifts we can offer one another. A soothing balm in human relationships, forgiveness restores mystery, human dignity and relatedness to another person or group of people. Everyone will experience hurt or betrayal in life. No one will be spared the experience. Whether in a schoolyard prank or through neglect, we will all feel the sting of betrayal and sin. *And, it hurts.* And whether we want to admit it or not, we too have sinned against others, causing harm, alienation and even exile.

Forgiveness repairs and restores. Forgiveness moves beyond differences. Forgiveness challenges our inner need to be justified, in control and self-righteous even in the face of downright evil and sin. A person who lives with a forgiving heart cares more for the inherent dignity, mercy and restoration of another person (even to the person causing harm) than they do for retribution. God has a desire to bring people into relatedness, into reconciliation with one another. The spiritual practice of forgiveness is not easy, even with Jesus inspiring and helping us along. Yet, it is only in forgiving that we truly encounter holy peace in mind, body and soul.

Our Western culture values retribution and punishment more than healing and restoration. In Middle Eastern culture a great emphasis is also placed upon retribution and honor. The actions of Jesus moved beyond any cultural norm creating a new order of forgiveness and mercy. When the disciples asked Jesus how many times they needed to forgive someone, they were surprised to hear the response: "Not seven times, but, I tell you, seventy-seven times." (Matthew 18:22b). In other words: *There is no limit to forgiveness.* And Jesus wasn't just speaking to his contemporaries; he was speaking to us too.

An authentic spiritual relationship calls us to accountability. We have to forgive the unforgivable with loving mercy. A spirituality of forgiveness invites every one of us to initiate acts of forgiveness. According to the teaching of Jesus, we ask another to forgive us personally when we have caused harm. We must forgive *everyone*, even if that someone who has harmed us is unaware of his actions. However, forgiveness does not imply a lack of accountability for the perpetrator's actions; rather, forgiveness is meant to free the one who is harmed from hate, bitterness and anger. The perpetrator, however, must do his part to right the wrong committed. This is known as restorative justice.[2] In other words, forgiving another does not mean one can remain in an abusive or unsafe situation or be a spiritual doormat. And just because you have forgiven another does not free the perpetrator or sinner of his obligation to repair and restore the damage done—to you and to himself.

Forgiveness is a tricky topic and psychologically and spiritually can become a brier nest if one's heart is not turned to God and prayer, especially when confronted by actions that seem too horrific to forgive. The right course of action might be stillness and prayer, not immediate pardon. God's grace will heal parts of ourselves that we never thought possible. Forgiveness and mercy change the forgiver and create interior space for healing to occur.

When we do not forgive, our hearts harden toward others and even ourselves. We create our own spiritual harm and stumbling blocks. We cause hurt to our own soul through continued negative, judgmental thoughts and actions. When we fail to forgive, we carry a heavy burden and gain a hardness of heart. The soil of our life becomes barren and rocky and our growth is stunted. In contrast, the act of forgiveness is a way to praise God and bless one another.

Finally, we must accept the forgiveness God seeks to offer to us and forgive ourselves. Spiritual healing occurs by our participation in a mutual love relationship of humble honesty with God. When we have experienced forgiveness—real forgiveness, not just lip service—we are more easily able to forgive and reconcile. Our presence becomes a healing solace for the world. Forgiveness begins in the human heart, dances into personal relationships, waltzes into communities and organizations and brings the promise of dialogue, reconciliation and peace.

MEDITATION
Breathe quietly for two minutes. Engage your senses, intuition and emotions to recall an unresolved situation or instance when you caused harm to another person. Enter into prayer using *lectio divina* with the following verses from Matthew:

> Then Peter came and said to him, "Lord, if another member
> of the church sins against me, how often should I forgive? As
> many as seven times?" Jesus said to him, "Not seven times,
> but, I tell you, seventy-seven times." (Matthew 18:21–22)

Conclude by discerning if an act of forgiveness and reconciliation can begin to flow from your prayer today. Sit in silence for one minute. Offer a prayer in your own words to God, gathering any insights awakened within you today.

Day 34: Gathering Fruit of Concern for the World

If you remove the yoke from among you,
    the pointing of the finger, the speaking of evil,
if you offer your food to the hungry
    and satisfy the needs of the afflicted,
then your light shall rise in the darkness
    and your gloom be like the noonday.
The LORD will guide you continually,
    and satisfy your needs in parched places,
    and make your bones strong;
and you shall be like a watered garden,
    like a spring of water,
    whose waters never fail. (Isaiah 58:9b–11)

Many gardeners' favorite perennial is the *Dicentra spectabilis*, commonly known as a bleeding heart. I planted two in the garden near the entrance of our home. When early spring arrives, the bleeding hearts are quick to show lacey leaves and long stems of strawberry-colored blossoms, some with as many as twenty dancing heart shapes on a stem. Each blossom is shaped like a heart. To pray with the image of bleeding heart flowers is to be reminded of how much suffering exists in our world. In full bloom, this stunning garden flower visually proclaims all our need for love and concern.

Today I invite you to gather the specific concerns of the world that touch and move your heart and emotion. For each of us, there is a purpose beyond ourselves that speaks directly to our soul and the world's great need. It might arise from of our past experiences, or the life we live now. One person cares for the elderly, lonely and homebound. Another is present to the physically abused. The plight of a war-ravaged country might speak to one, while a homeless person shivering with hunger and cold might call to someone else.

Both the Old and New Testament Scriptures convey a primary concern for the poor and marginalized. God addresses this concern more than any other topic. God's invitation is clear, and our action is not optional. But how do we choose where to focus our effort? The clue to the answer of this question is within each of us. How, when, where is our heart deeply moved? The suffering and pain in the world can be overwhelming, and some days it seems easier to do nothing. *How can one person make a difference?* The fact is that each action makes a difference. Interestingly, in our spiritual garden we discover that there is a home for everyone. Saint Vincent de Paul walked this path well, and he demonstrated to all of us the need to reach out beyond ourselves—to the materially poor and marginalized, for example—for a healthy spiritual life.

Your heart bleeds and cares for a stranger somewhere in the world. There is a social concern that grabs your heart and speaks to the longing in your soul for healing, hope and wholeness. You may already know how you are called to serve others. On the other hand, this could be the opportunity for you to finally hear your heart's innermost desires. Each person has a different call, a different concern. This is good. For example, I am drawn to service with children who suffer from abuse and neglect and to women who are violated by abusive power structures. In contrast, my husband's heart cries out when he encounters a person in need who is elderly or suffering with a physical disability. You, too, will have a particular population or issue that grabs your heart and will not let go. In your spiritual garden the tug of concern will not go away, and you must tend to it.

Next week you will spend more time exploring how your generosity and concern for others can overflow into service. Today calls simply for reflection. How is your heart pierced with concern for others? How do you gather concern for the world?

MEDITATION

Go to a garden or park. Find a quiet place to sit or walk slowly and peacefully.

Look around you. Notice the firmness of earth supporting you, the trees, vastness of the sky, perhaps a horizon. Become fully present. What grabs your attention? Stop and notice. Bring your attention to your breath. Allow your chest to slow into deep, rhythmic breaths, rising and falling in your body. Notice any scents or sounds. Pay attention to thoughts that arise in your mind. Gently let them pass. Connect to the world. Imagine the diversity of people inhabiting the earth on multiple continents. Realize that what affects one person, affects you. Continue breathing.

Reflect upon the current world news and ask God to bring an image to your mind of what or who is in most need of your care, your concern, your love, your presence. Listen to what commands your attention.

Allow your heart to expand with whatever person, image or concern that rises within you. Breathe stillness, asking God to brand your heart with love. Make a silent commitment to allow a deeper consciousness to rise within you for the person, population or issue that grabbed your heart.

Conclude with five minutes of journaling in order to articulate your thoughts.

Day 35: Gathering Fruits

Place yourself deliberately in God's presence and breathe quietly, stilling your mind.

Thoughts of gathering have accompanied your prayer and activity for the past six days. Beginning with gathering the beauty of the ordinary in the everyday, you reflected upon how you show up for all of your life. A day of play and leisure was hopefully rejuvenating. Perhaps it illuminated your desire to create more sacred spaces for spending time deliberately with God. Further reflections revolved around naming the values and principles you stake your life upon. You spent time praying with forgiveness: of receiving forgiveness, offering healing balm for the world. Lastly you gathered a concern in your heart for the world. Your life is a beautiful bouquet that reveals the inner beauty and outer action of your essence, scenting others with pleasure and gift. Truly you are becoming a spiritual gardener of depth and vitality.

MEDITATION

Take your gardening tool and seed packet and place them in your hands.

Slowly pray Matthew 13:18–23, the Scripture that began your week of gathering the fruits of your life.

Ponder the last line. How does it reveal to you the fruits of your life in relationship to your week's reflection?

How is the gardening tool speaking to you symbolically about a week of gathering?

Choose a physical activity to stretch your body so you can appreciate the container for all your blossoming and fullness of life!

Conclude by reflecting about how your presence touches the hearts of those around you.

WEEK SIX: GENEROUS GIFTS

The only way I can prove my love is by scattering flowers and these flowers are every little sacrifice, every glance and word, and the doing of the least of actions for love. I wish both to suffer and to find joy through love. Thus I will scatter my flowers.[1]

—Thérèse of Lisieux

He who supplies seed to the sower and bread for food will supply and multiply your seed for sowing and increase the harvest of your righteousness. You will be enriched in every way for your great generosity, which will produce thanksgiving to God through us; for the rendering of this ministry not only supplies the needs of the saints but also overflows with many thanksgivings to God.
(2 Corinthians 9:10–12)

Today I curl up in a blue velvet chair, in a room overflowing with books and photographs where I pray, write and spiritually accompany others. Last week a large, unexpected package arrived from my mother. Surprised and delighted, I received the gift of a family treasure: an afghan my grandmother had made fifty years ago. To guard against the snowy cold of the day, I wrap myself in crème-colored wool, stitched with plate-sized pink roses in vertical patterns. Though grandma died nearly twenty years ago, on this day I feel embraced by roses from the garden of her love she so generously shared with her family, evident in this special blanket, completed stitch by stitch.

I discovered a love for flowers while visiting my grandparents. I was delighted to find gardens lush with irises, roses, day lilies and other assorted perennials. *Didn't everyone know that vegetable gardens were planted so children could play hide and seek?*

And zucchinis were grown to provide imaginary baby dolls? Throughout summer I could smell sweet peas, which perfumed the air as I fell into sleep. Through these gardens and the gardeners I loved, a deep sense of belonging and generosity enveloped my spirit and remained with me.

The entire world receives a gift from the spiritual gardens and generosity of others. When we use our time, attention, talent and treasure to help our families, communities and individuals on the margins, we have the opportunity to greet God and discover a taste of the kingdom that God desires for our world.

The generosity of others blesses and sanctifies. Have you ever experienced a gift that is unearned and unexpected? Do you find yourself completely surprised, even speechless, and simply filled with gratitude and astonishment? This is exactly how God wants to delight every one of us, and how we are invited to give ourselves away for others. The sun and moon give themselves away to all of creation. Jesus offered his life for the sake of the world. Some great historical figures offer us examples of love and service. Family members or friends may also be committed to a person or cause and share their time and treasures. We too are called to give ourselves away to someone and for something that matters to our soul.

It is unfortunate that in our Western culture, we base our spirituality on principles of entitlement and what we can "get out of" someone or something, in other words, *transactional spirituality*. The idea of transactional spirituality is dangerous. In a mature spirituality our actions originate from love, concern and care—directives straight from the Christian Scriptures. We do not act from self-motivation or a disordered impulse. Our deeds and actions must begin with a rooting in a primary love relationship with God and flow from that place of blessing. We do not act because we think our acts will be rewarded or punished.

Perhaps an idea such as this may be a motivator in the early stages of the spiritual journey, but no person should remain in or perpetuate an immature understanding of God's love in this way.

The concept of spiritual generosity is the polar opposite of entitlement or transactional spirituality. Goodness flows from generosity and the unconditional love of the giver. A giver gives to others because he can. A gift may be as simple as acknowledgment of another person, by really seeing a person. Someone can offer his life in service of others through his primary vocation, whether it is to educate, relieve suffering or even found a nonprofit that benefits others. Generosity is so simple, but we humans make it immensely complex through our egos and fear.

Though generosity can flow from overabundance, real spiritual generosity flows from a primary spiritual grounding in hope. An initial spiritual orientation of scarcity causes hoarding, fear and resentment. Trusting that God and the universe are conspiring for life and love helps to open our very being to meaning, simplicity and gratitude. A spiritual gardener is, through the thrust of a generous life force, designed to see the world with a different set of eyes and a heart of purity.

This final week of your retreat will be spent praying with generosity of your talents, time and treasure and a sense of poverty. You will listen for the silent whisper and abundant love of the Divine in the midst of your daily life, home, workplace and in the world. You will have an opportunity to identify a sacred name for yourself, create a daily prayer for your life and determine a legacy that you want to share with others. Throughout the week you will become attentive to thanksgiving and praise for the God that creates, heals, redeems and bestows life, inviting you to do the same!

PEONY

Peony has bloomed, bringing delight to the small corner of garden life. True to herself, she has provided sweetness and beauty to the world. If she could speak, perhaps we would hear her testament in words such as these that follow.

"My name is Peony, Paeonia lactiflora, rosea plena, to be precise. I have lived the past six years in a small flowerbed with my friends of oregano, thyme, iris and rose. A tall neighboring tree provides afternoon shade beginning in late May, just after I have bloomed. Early in the season I begin to flower since my home is next to the house foundation. Everyone seems to admire my short-lived blooms. Occasionally someone cuts one of my blossoms and takes it indoors to become the centerpiece at a family meal or on a prayer table. Other times butterflies, birds and bees flit around me and occasionally stop for a brief visit.

"When the heat of the summer passes, golden leaves pile near my stems, and a season of visible growth passes. I ready myself for winter and conserve energy. Gradually leaves blow away, and my caretaker cuts my dying stems to the ground. As earth freezes, the master gardener makes certain my crown and eye nodules have not been covered by soil and mulch. I rest in the quiet. Birds chirp their good-byes, rains cease and snow blankets the land. Then soon, once again, sun thaws the hardened earth and clouds rain water into my roots. My master gardener returns and fertilizes me with blood and bone meal, and my energy stirs me toward growth and bloom. I give myself away, anew.

"I hold a place of privilege, for someone loves, notices and tends me with care. And in return, I am life-giving to others.

"I hope that my story has helped illuminate your journey of growth and discovery."

Day 36: Generosity

Jacob said, "No, please; if I find favor with you, then accept my present from my hand; for truly to see your face is like seeing the face of God—since you have received me with such favor. Please accept my gift that is brought to you, because God has dealt graciously with me, and because I have everything I want." So he urged him, and he took it. (Genesis 33:10–11)

Many people form us and give us their time, talents, mercy and treasures. The memory of a teacher or mentor who spent time helping us to learn—a coach, spouse, parent or stranger may come to mind. Our families, friends, faith communities, institutions and God give us a generous legacy. Our religious and spiritual inheritance and ultimate gift of life is beyond measure.

When you hold one small seed in your hand, it is challenging to comprehend that ultimately something much more will grow and flourish from within the little and almost invisible seed. The gardener holds so much hope when planting a garden. And God, parents, mentors and others also hold hope for each one of us while marveling at our smallness, beauty and potential!

Today will be spent recognizing how others have wrapped you with generosity, and how you have shared generously. Perhaps your meditation will cause you to remember an individual offering you encouragement, support or even a meal. Maybe you or someone you know has been the recipient of a generous organization, offering of aid or even political asylum.

MEDITATION
Breathe quietly for five minutes, gathering your mind, heart and body to stillness.

Allow a memory of a time when someone showered you with generosity to come into your heart and mind. Enter into your memory using your senses and imagination and touch the core emotions that the experience brought to you.

Record in your journal for a few minutes about anything that emerges for you, especially thoughts and actions that you want to remember with gratitude.

Now allow a second memory to come into your heart and mind. This time remember a time when you shared your generosity. Enter into your memory using your senses and imagination and touch the core emotions that the experience brought to you. Add to your journal, recalling any thoughts and insights that surface within you.

Finally, sit in stillness and ask the Holy Spirit to reveal a situation inviting you to greater generosity. Pay attention to the situation, people and responses that arise within you. Listen for clarity. What do you experience in your heart, mind and body?

Write in your journal one more time and commit yourself to being open to the personal invitation to be more generous.

Conclude by finding your pulse in your wrist, resting for three minutes or longer in gratitude for God's overflowing generosity of life.

Day 37: Generous Love

After this there was a festival of the Jews, and Jesus went up to Jerusalem.

Now in Jerusalem by the Sheep Gate there is a pool, called in Hebrew Beth-zatha, which has five porticoes. In these lay many invalids—blind, lame, and paralyzed. One man was there who had been ill for thirty-eight years. When Jesus saw him lying there and knew that he had been there a long time, he said to him, "Do you want to be made well?" The sick man answered him, "Sir, I have no one to put me into the pool when the water is stirred up; and while I am making my way, someone else steps down ahead of me." Jesus said to him, "Stand up, take your mat and walk." At once the man was made well, and he took up his mat and began to walk.

Now that day was a sabbath. (John 5:1–9)

There is no experience quite like being the recipient of generous love and presence from another person, even a stranger. The times in our life when we experience complete acceptance by another creates within ourselves powerful interior freedom. The demands and insistent voices within us become calm and our breathing slows. We experience a more rhythmic heartbeat, and we feel an interconnection with others. This interplay can occur with the Beloved, the known or with a complete stranger—at any time, in any place. Encounters with personal, real presence are life-giving, perhaps surprising and fulfilling, and are transformative for the giver and receiver.

How do you give yourself away to others in a way that is meaningful and delightful? First, you give yourself away by knowing the "yes" of your life, and what values are most important to you. Knowing these offer you clarity and the ability to be present and engaged.

Second, you have identified the concern that grabs your heart. For example, on day thirty-four you had identified a world issue that spoke to you personally and invited you to action.

Third, you have entered into prayer to ask for clarity, and you have listened to how God responds to your very specific life situation in the details. Finally, you have made a decision and a plan of action to respond to the person or situation that grabs your soul, and who needs the gift of your presence, love and action.

Several years ago, while leading a week service-immersion trip with college students, I realized I was searching in all the wrong places for how to offer my life in direct relationship and service to others in need. It suddenly dawned on me that I did not need to look any further than the very life I was already living. At the time, my husband and I had opened our home and hearts to a young homeless boy. I didn't need a retreat or to even search elsewhere to be present to the materially poor and marginalized. Surprise! I already had an orphan living in my home!

You too might discover something similar. Are you already serving another? Perhaps all that you need to do is to see with a new set of eyes and an expanded vision.

When considering where you might volunteer, you have to make some distinctions. You can become involved in an event that will benefit someone or something, through a charity or a service organization. Or you can choose to be in direct contact— face-to-face and in relationship with a stranger or person in need. Both are noble calls. However, serving others directly is true generosity. Jesus invites us to this over and over in the Gospels. The surprise that occurs time and again for people of all ages is something like this: "I thought I was serving...but I received so much more than I gave." This demonstrates the mysterious power of care and generosity we encounter in service. In essence, when we become a nourishing presence for someone else, we realize that we have been transformed and humbled ourselves.

As an aside—or perhaps incentive—it is interesting to note that recent medical studies have revealed that volunteering face-to-face actually boosts your immune system and increases wellness for individuals and organizations.[2] When Jesus healed the man in the Scripture reading for today, he was healing someone whom others had ignored. We receive the same invitation to respond to the human persons on the fringe of our society and communities, and in the process we increase our own spiritual well-being and health!

MEDITATION

Breathe quietly in God's presence. Enter into the *lectio divina* process (outlined on pages 26–27) with John 5:1–9.

Write in your journal any insights you become aware of, and then reflect upon the following questions and record any insights:

- Who repels me? What population am I least inclined to interact with? Think of: race, gender, social and economic status, religious affiliation, sexual orientation, ability and age.
- Is there a person already in my life whom I might need to see with new eyes?
- How might God invite me to overcome my initial inclinations or aversion with a generous outpouring of love and kindness?

Conclude with a prayer from your own heart, in your own words.

Day 38: Generous Talent

Then the one who had received the five talents came forward, bringing five more talents, saying, "Master, you handed over to me five talents; see, I have made five more talents." His master said to him, "Well done, good and trustworthy slave; you have been trustworthy in a few things, I will put you in charge of many things; enter into the joy of your master." And the one with the two talents also came forward, saying, "Master, you handed over to me two talents; see, I have made two more talents." His master said to him, "Well done, good and trustworthy slave; you have been trustworthy in a few things, I will put you in charge of many things; enter into the joy of your master." (Matthew 25:20–23)

Talents offer a gateway into full participation within the kingdom of God, here and now. Faithful development and use of the talents seeded within ourselves allows contribution and participation in creating abundant life for the world. We have spent time praying with the things that bring us joy and the passion and actions that make us come alive! God does not give us talents for our own pleasure and purpose, rather God give us talents primarily to serve the world in simple and generous ways.

As talents grow and shift throughout our life, so do the ways we use our talents. Like the servant in the Scripture today, we learn that eventually greater responsibility and joy come through the cultivation of our gifts. We have the choice to exercise talents or allow them to wither and die. Similar to a garden in bloom, our talents can flourish and then outgrow the places we allow them to occupy. We must not be fearful to seek the new and unknown horizon where our talents can be magnified and expanded.

One day I realized that I needed to divide and transplant the daylilies and bearded irises in my garden, which had grown to the edge of the terraced boundaries. I did manage to divide and transplant the daylilies. But then my life became too busy and I missed the opportunity to transplant the irises. A year later the irises did not flower. I waited too long. Lesson learned. However, the vibrant orange daylilies that I transplanted still thrive and add splashes of color in their new locations. Like the daylilies, at times we must move, spread out and grow in order to share our talents with others. And when our talents grow, they become a glittering gold gift that we bestow upon humanity. They also enlarge our capacity to love and participate in life.

Whether we share ourselves with the world through the creative arts, sciences, social sciences, humanities, sports, relational endeavors, gardening or simply by loving others, God reveals the kingdom of heaven and comes alive in our lives.

MEDITATION

Breathe gently for five minutes, and pay attention to where your mind and heart wander.

Reflect with the following questions:

- How do you share your talents? Are you like the daylilies, willing to move to new places, spreading your roots to thrive and grow? Or are you more like the irises—in a space too cramped for your beauty and gifts—and unable to make a change?
- How can your talents benefit your own well-being and the places you frequent most often?
- Identify three or more talents you possess and can share with others.

At the end of the day, spend some time with the following creative meditation. Allow one or more talents to surface in your mind. Reflect on one of these talents, and allow the talent to speak to you in the first person. Does it reveal how it wants to participate in your world? Record in your journal what you discover.

In the next twenty-four hours, share with a safe person (one who will not judge you and from whom you can receive an honest perspective) what you have discovered about yourself and your talents. What talents does he or she think you possess? Are you surprised by his or her response?

PRAYER

Do not fear, for heaven is near, waiting with a sigh of delight, a generous unfolding.

Day 39: Generous Treasure

As for those who in the present age are rich, command them not to be haughty, or to set their hopes on the uncertainty of riches, but rather on God who richly provides us with everything for our enjoyment. They are to do good, to be rich in good works, generous, and ready to share, thus storing up for themselves the treasure of a good foundation for the future, so that they may take hold of the life that really is life. (1 Timothy 6:17–19)

Regardless of a joyful or an abusive childhood, we all had hopes and dreams at one point in our young life. Throughout our teen years we developed our dreams in spite of voices in the world attempting to intrude upon our deepest desires. As we entered into our young adult years, we made decisions that may have resulted in permanent commitments. The actions we took based on our decisions may have resulted in positive life directions or may have resulted in serious consequences. In either case, we probably gained a deeper understanding of our life's purpose with each decision we made.

Whatever your age, today finds you with a treasure chest of hopes and dreams. Hopefully you have realized many of the dreams you held as a child. But perhaps you still experience a longing for unrealized treasures that reside in your heart. One way you can realize your dreams is if you identify your vocation in life and begin to share that vocation with others—through your time, talent, values and good works. Knowing your identity and calling allows you to give others your material and spiritual treasures and, in the meantime, realize your dreams.

Each of us has one distinct life to live. On our life journey we will suffer, laugh, love passionately and give ourselves to a purpose. We will discover our lives are interwoven with one another and that we are called to respond generously to those in need. We offer mercy to the world with our resources and treasures that multiply over time. To help us determine our vocation and how we can generously share our treasures, we can choose a *sacred name* or symbol that will guide, nourish, shelter and awaken the deep desires and dreams within us.

Many years ago, after discerning I was not called to a permanent vocation in religious life, I made promises to a Carmelite community as a laywoman and added a spiritual name to my birth name. My chosen name, Margaret Ann of Corpus Christi, is included in a prayer I composed and pray with daily. When discerning identity and purpose, the name acts as a guide. Similarly, sometimes I use a symbol (not just a name) to understand who I am, and what role or place I have in the world. Some images that I use include, but are not limited to, the bee, lighthouse and fireweed plant. By *sacred naming*, or using of other names and symbols to describe myself, I gain a deeper understanding of who I am and of whom God dreams me to become.

Today you will begin the process of discovering a sacred name for yourself. A sacred name will broaden and deepen your notion of the divine and your relationship with God.

MEDITATION

Locate a variety of photographs from your life. Slowly look over the pictures with eyes of love. Begin to imagine yourself as a treasure in the heart of God. What gifts does your life reveal? What images reflect the person you are today? Now take some time to reflect upon what your unique sacred name is or could be. Throughout history, many ordinary and holy people have taken names that help shape their identity. Catholics pray with names in litanies throughout the liturgical year. What symbol from the created world or attribute of the Divine speaks deeply to your soul? A symbol or name can change and evolve over time and is unique to the specifics in your life, yet draws you into mystery and potential of what could be. Allow a variety of images and names to resonate and speak to your essence. You'll know when you hear or recognize your sacred name. A sacred name can be intimidating, challenging and may open you to the possibility of deeper transformation and mercy toward others. A sacred name can reveal how God may be choosing to speak to you. The process will take time, and it is only a beginning.

When the time comes that a symbol seems to want to stay with you, spend some creative time drawing, painting, journaling or even singing with the symbol. Do what best fits you and your personality. Look for pictures, images and words. Use your imagination and prayer to see how your sacred name speaks to you and thus the world. It may take weeks or months to determine what name depicts who you are in the world and invites you to action.

Conclude by pondering the Scripture for the day in your heart.

Day 40: Generous Poverty

"I am deeply grieved, even to death; remain here and keep awake." And going a little farther, he threw himself on the ground and prayed that, if it were possible, the hour might pass from him. He said, "Abba, Father, for you all things are possible; remove this cup from me; yet, not what I want, but what you want." (Mark 14:34-36)

Pain and suffering are part of the human condition. At some point, we will all experience physical, psychological or spiritual trauma, loss or darkness. Like the grain of wheat that must die, ultimately we too must experience bodily death. But our greatest poverty lies not in death, but rather, not living fully present to resurrection and hope.

The cross of Jesus offers meaning to our suffering. In the garden of Gethsemane we discover we are not alone in our anguish. As Christians, when we stand at the foot of the cross, we also know of the hope of an empty tomb in a garden of promise. When we feel we are nailed to the cross and persecuted, God is already present with us, having gone to where we would rather not go. Our wounds take time—even a lifetime—to heal. The fireweed flower rises from burnt ash; a tree takes root in a rock crack. Compost provides new life for growing and established plants. Hope exists for the gardener of our soul to transform even the deadliest suffering into generous life and gift.

There are reasons why pain, suffering and poverty exist in the world. The choice is to realize that we are not alone. When we suffer, our hands reach out to grasp the unseen God in our family, community and even with the stranger. Even then, it can seem as if there is no relief, no answer big enough, no grace in the world. It is then that we must not question why, and instead, leap into the abyss of God's holy embrace. There we will learn we are not alone. A tender welcome and reconciling embrace extends across all division and greets us by name.

Healing, hope and promise are generously shared. Our only response in return is generous self-emptying and transformation. There is no other way to joy except through the cross and resurrection. Generous poverty or sacrifice lead us to joy and truth. There is no absence of light in darkness. The dawning sun will always rise. Wounds transform to gifts. God offers salvation and hope to all.

MEDITATION

Sit in silence. You are not alone.

Spend fifteen minutes simply becoming aware of your breathing. Disregard any thoughts that push into your consciousness.

After fifteen minutes pass, reflect on your inner poverty. How can you be led to share your life with others through wounds and poverty?

PRAYER

Add to this eucharistic prayer in your own words:

Dear _____

Take me _____

Bless me _____

Break me of _____

Give me as _____

Amen.

Day 41: Generous Legacy

Finally, all of you, have unity of spirit, sympathy, love for one another, a tender heart, and a humble mind. Do not repay evil for evil or abuse for abuse; but, on the contrary, repay with a blessing. It is for this that you were called— that you might inherit a blessing. For

"Those who desire life
   and desire to see good days,
let them keep their tongues from evil
   and their lips from speaking deceit;
let them turn away from evil and do good;
   let them seek peace and pursue it...." (1 Peter 3:8–11)

How do you desire to be known in the world? What is the legacy you wish to leave when your time on earth comes to an end?

Jesus left a powerful legacy to us: He asked that we love one another and live with peace and mercy. His life was his testament. In the Gospel of John, Jesus promised that we would do even greater things than he did. It is possible, through our willingness to grow and let go of fear, to surrender to God with love and humble gratitude.

In all likelihood, you can think of hundreds of people who have lived inspiring lives with a commitment to justice, holiness, integrity and love. The example of Saint Thérèse of Lisieux is only one of many.

Thérèse, a young Carmelite nun who lived in France from 1873 to 1897, loved gardens. Thérèse is most commonly known as "the Little Flower." Some mistake her spirituality as inordinately pious and unrealistic for today's world. In reality, the Little Flower demonstrated profound generosity. She had one desire—to simply love God and to send a shower of roses to earth after her death. Thérèse made a generous promise that while in heaven she would continue to do good work on earth, showering an outpouring of generous love to all. Thérèse demonstrated a movement from selfish preoccupation to selfless love and an outpouring for others. She, like many others, offers a legacy that is as uniquely personal as it is universal.

MEDITATION

Find your pulse, hold it and breathe in stillness for five minutes.

Go for a walk outdoors. Today you will begin to write a personal prayer that embodies your life and the legacy you wish to offer to the world. Ponder these questions:

- Who inspires me?
- What five qualities do I value above all others?
- Who are the people that need me?

- Where are my talents, passion and treasure most deeply engaged?
- What do I bring to almost every situation?
- What specific areas about life arouse and inspire me?
- How does God invite me to love more deeply?
- Where do I discover my longing and need for wonder, humility and generosity?
- When am I fearful and lonely?
- If I were nearing the end of my life, what is the legacy my life can offer?

As you walk, ponder these questions and any others that surface for you. When you return, begin to compose a personal prayer that you will be able to pray each day. Ultimately, your prayer will articulate the desire of your soul, your gifts and poverty, and incarnate truth and meaning.

Day 42: Generous Gifts

Place yourself deliberately in God's presence and breathe quietly and still your mind.

Take your gardening tool and seed packet and place them in your hands.

Slowly pray 2 Corinthians 9:10–12, the Scripture that began your week of reflection about generosity.

Slowly review your week. Reflect upon your journal entries and daily reflections about where you offer and experience generosity and gifts. Ask yourself the following questions reflecting upon your life as it has been revealed to you this week:

- Where am I encountering God in my daily life?
- Am I inspired in any way?
- How has generosity become more evident in my life the past six weeks?

- Have I become aware of any lack of interior freedom?
- What has matured in me? Are there ways I give myself away to others?
- What type of garden does my life evoke in me? Describe it.

Spend time pondering the symbol you chose for yourself or composing your personal prayer.

Record in your journal any insights, thoughts or feelings you experience. Conclude by pondering how your sacrifices, glances, words and actions resemble a scattering of beautiful flowers in a spiritual garden.

BEYOND SIX WEEKS: CLOSING RITUAL AND COVENANT

LOCATION
Determine ahead of time a location to conclude your retreat. You will need to plan on approximately one hour for this closing ritual. Perhaps return to the place where your retreat started with your opening ritual.

SUPPLIES
You will need your hand-gardening tool, package of seeds, journal, pen, original retreat covenant, blank paper for a new covenant and the personal prayer you composed during week six.

OPENING SCRIPTURE
> O you who dwell in the gardens,
>> my companions are listening for your voice;
>> let me hear it. (Song of Solomon 8:13)

OPENING PRAYER
> *Master Gardener, you created the world and desire that I love you with all my mind, heart and soul. Thank you for cultivating my ability to love you more intentionally with all of who I am.*
>
> *Master Gardener, you are already present in every moment of my daily life. Thank you for teaching me to discover and appreciate your presence in the people and places I encounter every day.*
>
> *Master Gardener, you will come alive more fully in my life when I surrender to your loving will and design for my life that we create together. Allow me to continue to give you permission to transform me through love, suffering and delight all the days of my life.*

SCRIPTURE MEDITATION

Slowly read and meditate on the following Scripture verses:

> In the beginning was the Word, and the Word was with God, and the Word was God. He was in the beginning with God. All things came into being through him, and without him not one thing came into being. What has come into being in him was life, and the life was the light of all people. (John 1:1–4)

REFLECTION

What has come alive in your soul and life the past six weeks?

SCRIPTURE

> The eyes of the Lord are on those who love him,
>   a mighty shield and strong support,
> a shelter from scorching wind and a shade from noonday
>   sun,
>   a guard against stumbling and a help against falling.
> He lifts up the soul and makes the eyes sparkle;
>   he gives health and life and blessing. (Sirach 34:19–20)

REFLECTION

How are your eyes a sparkling reflection of your spiritual garden?

SCRIPTURE

> The Spirit and the bride say, "Come."
> And let everyone who hears say, "Come."
> And let everyone who is thirsty come.
> Let anyone who wishes take the water of life as a gift.
> (Revelation 22:17)

CLOSING REFLECTION

Think about the ways you have been re-created throughout this retreat. How have you tended to your spiritual garden and to the presence of God? What have you noticed? Are there changes that have occurred within you? How has the Holy One worked in secret, watering your soul and senses? If you could distill your retreat into one or two thoughts, what words or images would you choose?

Hold your gardening tool. Ponder it closely. What has this instrument come to represent to you over the past forty-two days? How has this simple implement assisted you in your desire for a deeper spiritual life, offering you answers to questions, and helped you to understand what you did not know you already knew?

Speak aloud to your gardening implement, as if it had a life of its own and was a close personal friend. Talk about your gratitude for your retreat and what you unearthed.

Now take your chosen seed packet in your hands. Look at the image of the matured seed on the front of the packet and planting guidelines on the back of the packet. How have these seeds grown throughout the retreat? Contemplate one seed. How can that one seed represent the continued hope God has for you right now and in the future? Sit quietly for as long as you desire. Make a decision about what you want to do with your seeds. Decide if you want to scatter your seeds into the wind, plant them, give them to a friend or gardener or keep them as a reminder of your continued growth. Record any insights in your journal.

Finally, reflect upon each gift of the Holy Spirit in Galatians 5:22–23a, and in your journal contemplate one way that each has been evident in your life these past six weeks.

The fruit of love _____

The fruit of joy _____

The fruit of peace _____

The fruit of patience _____

The fruit of kindness _____

The fruit of generosity _____

The fruit of faithfulness _____

The fruit of gentleness _____

The fruit of self-control _____

CLOSING PRAYER

Offer thanksgiving to God in your own words.

FINAL COVENANT

With prayerful attentiveness, review the elements of your old covenant and create a new covenant for the coming days, weeks and year of your life. Only choose what will be life-giving to you. Write your choices in ink. When you are finished, pray:

> For the mountains may depart and the hills be removed,
> but my steadfast love shall not depart from you,
>> and my covenant of peace shall not be removed,
>> says the LORD, who has compassion on you.
> (Isaiah 54:10)

Acknowledge the steadfast love and presence offered to you. In silence breathe until you experience a sense of inner peace. Imagine peace flowing from your heart into the physical area surrounding you, then to the country you are in, then the continent you inhabit and finally around all the earth. Take as much time as you desire.

Pray the prayer aloud that you composed on *Day 41: Generous Legacy.*

CONCLUSION

> I therefore, the prisoner in the Lord, beg you to lead a life worthy of the calling to which you have been called, with all humility and gentleness, with patience, bearing with one another in love, making every effort to maintain the

unity of the Spirit in the bond of peace. There is one body and one Spirit, just as you were called to the one hope of your calling, one Lord, one faith, one baptism, one God and Father of all, who is above all and through all and in all. (Ephesians 4:1–6)

Amen!

NOTES

PREPARATIONS

[1] To locate a spiritual director near you, contact your local church or Spiritual Directors International at www.sdiworld.org.

[2] Contact the author if you would like help locating a spiritual director that can be available to you through E-mail or telephone: Pegge@PeggeBernecker.com.

OPENING RITUAL

[1] Pope John XXIII (Angelo Giuseppe Roncalli), *Lettere = Giovanni XXIII, Lettere 1958-1963* Fr. Loris Capovilla, ed. (Loreto, Italy: 1948), p. 481.

Fr. Loris Capovilla, who was Pope John XXIII's personal secretary (now Archbishop emeritus of Loreto, Italy) collected the private and public letters of John XXIII and published them in 1978 under the title "Lettere = Giovanni XXIII, Lettere 1958-1963." Upon hearing of the death of Pope Pius XII, October 9, 1958, John wrote in his diary: "Sister death came quickly and swiftly fulfilled her office." On Sunday, October 9, at 3:52 A.M., Pius XII was in paradise. One of my favorite phrases brings me great comfort: "We are not on earth as museum-keepers, but to cultivate a flourishing garden of life and to prepare a glorious future. The Pope is dead, long live the Pope!" (*Lettere*, p. 481).

[2] Pope John XXIII, p. 481.

WEEK ONE: GROUND OF MY GARDEN

[1] Julian of Norwich, *Revelations of Divine Love*. Clinton Wolters, trans. (Great Britain: Penguin Classics, 1966) section 56, p. 161.

[2] Paula D'Arcy is a retreat leader and author. In September 2004 she gave a talk at Creator Mundi in Denver, Colorado. I had the opportunity to speak with her personally and ask where in her writing I could find this quote I had heard attributed to her. She explained it was not in writing anywhere—yet! I asked if I could quote her for a book I was writing, and she smiled and answered, "Of course." Paula can be contacted through her Web site: www.RedBirdFoundation.com.

WEEK TWO: PLANTING SEEDS

[1] Padre Pio, *Saint Padre Pio of Pietrelcina, Italy* (Miami Beach, Fla.: Vincent Falco, 1994), p. 17.

WEEK THREE: TENDING THE GARDEN

[1] Saint Teresa of Avila, *The Collected Works of St. Teresa of Avila*, volume 1, revised edition, Kieran Kavanaugh, O.C.D., and Otilio Rodriguez, O.C.D., trans. (Washington, D.C.: ICS, 1987), p. 137.

[2] The Myers-Briggs Type Indicator® is a helpful tool for understanding ourselves and those we live and work with. For more information about the Myers-Briggs Type Indicator®, visit the Web site: www.myersbriggs.org.

[3] For further reading on the subject, consider: Lynne Twist, *The Soul of Money* (New York: W.W. Norton & Company, 2003). Also, visit www.cfsaw.org. Vie Thorgren, D.MIN., is the executive director of The Center for Spirituality at Work in Denver, Colorado. Doctor Thorgren gives workshops and presentations about money myths.

WEEK FOUR: PRUNING AND APPRECIATING

[1] *Francis de Sales, Jane de Chantal: Letters of Spiritual Direction*, introduction by Wendy M. Wright and Joseph F. Power, O.S.F.S., *Classics of Western Spirituality* (Mahwah, N.J.: Paulist,

1986), pp. 202-203, as quoted in Bridget Mary Meehan, s.s.c., *Praying with Passionate Women* (New York: Crossroad, 1995), p. 104.

[2] Among many classical and contemporary writers, Franciscan priest Richard Rohr offers insight into a spirituality for the two halves of life with specific reference to the need for a "container" in the early years of one's life. A recommended CD of a retreat that explores these concepts further is: Richard Rohr, o.f.m., and Paula D'Arcy, *A Spirituality for the Two Halves of Life* (Cincinnati: St. Anthony Messenger Press, 2004).

WEEK FIVE: GATHERING FRUITS

[1] Vincent de Paul, "The Life of the Venerable Servant of God, Vincent de Paul," (1664): Chapter 5, as quoted in André Dodin, c.m., *Vincent de Paul and Charity* (New Rochelle, N.Y.: New City Press, 1993), p. 99.

[2] To learn more about restorative justice, visit www.restorative-justice.org or do your own Internet search for thousands of sites. I was introduced to the process of restorative justice in 2002 by Tom Cavanagh, a humble man who is a leading researcher and proponent of restorative justice.

WEEK SIX: GENEROUS GIFTS

[1] Thérèse of Lisieux, *The Autobiography of St. Thérèse of Lisieux: The Story of a Soul*, John Beevers, trans. (Garden City, N.Y.: Image, 1957), p. 156.

[2] A great online reference for excellent articles about spirituality and health is www.spiritualityhealth.com.